TWO of US

TWO of US

The Story of a Father, a Son, and
 THE BEATLES

Peter Smith

HOUGHTON MIFFLIN COMPANY

Boston • New York • 2004

For information about permission to reproduce selections
from this book, write to Permissions, Houghton Mifflin Company,
215 Park Avenue South, New York, New York 10003.

Visit our Web site: www.houghtonmifflinbooks.com.

Library of Congress Cataloging-in-Publication Data
Smith, Peter, date.
　Two of us : the story of a father, a son, and the Beatles / Peter Smith.
　　p.　cm.
　　ISBN 0-618-25145-6
　1. Smith, Peter, 1959– 2. Fathers and sons—Biography. 3. Rock
　　music fans—Biography. 4. Beatles. I. Title.
HQ755.85.S57 2004
306.874'2—dc22 2003056700

Book design by Melissa Lotfy

Printed in the United States of America

MAP 10 9 8 7 6 5 4 3 2 1

This book is for Sam, in the hopes he may enjoy remembering these days someday — and in memory of his grandfather.

Contents

I say in speeches that a plausible mission
of artists is to make people appreciate
being alive at least a little bit. I am then
asked if I know of any artists who pulled
that off. I reply, "The Beatles."

— KURT VONNEGUT

The Beatles will just go on and on . . .
the Beatles, I think, exist without us.

— GEORGE HARRISON

TWO of US

1.
Meet
the
Beatles

MY SON —handsome, kind, tall for his age, with a stickler's way of talking and a supernatural memory for raw data—was in the grip of his first-ever love affair. Not with his homeroom teacher. Not with the little dark-haired girl down the block. It wasn't a crush; crushes flowered in private, then wilted. It was less creepy, surer-footed than any obsession. Nor was it exclusive—other kids, I knew, shared his preoccupation.

No, more than three decades after their 1970 liquidation, Sam had fallen in love with the Beatles, a band that had burned out less than a decade after its founding, that had released only ten hours of music. In retrospect, it was easy to see why Sam's seven-year-old mind had locked onto the Beatles franchise, with its boyhood friendships and grownup squabbles, its rivalries, love affairs, submarines, octopuses, silver hammers, newspaper taxis, piggies, raccoons, meter maids, bulldogs, and shadowy Paul-is-dead clues. Making lists—compiling and comparing by letter and category a little slice of the world—has always seemed to me an especially male preoccupation. The uninterrupted dream that is the Beatles universe lends itself to endless poring over and mapping out. For Sam, it served as a way to bring coherence to something elusive and overwhelming: music, and how it made him feel; and life, as he was starting to understand what it gives and grabs away from you.

Nowhere were the Beatles more obsessively alive than in Sam's conversation, beginning first thing most weekday mornings and ending at eight or nine at night. At around 7 A.M., he would pad into our bedroom, wrap himself in a blanket, and lie stiffly breathing at the end of the bed, patiently rehearsing and rearranging various lyrics, characters, and VH1 *Behind the Music* storylines in his head. Then finally, it came out: "Dad—did you know what Paul called 'Yesterday' when he was writing it?"

"No, I'm not sure," I said, still half asleep.

"'Scrambled Eggs.' He wrote it with the words, 'Scrambled eggs / Oh, baby, how I love your legs.' Then he changed the title to 'Yesterday' later on."

"Wow. I'm not sure 'Scrambled Eggs' would've worked out."

"Why would somebody love somebody else's legs?"

"It . . . happens."

Just as I was drifting back to sleep, the voice would blurt again: "Dad?"

"Uh-huh . . . ?"

"You know John and Paul?"

"Uh-huh . . . ?"

"How many songs do you think Paul wrote, and how many songs do you think John wrote—of all the songs the Beatles sang in all?"

"I don't know. Paul wrote thirty and John wrote thirty-five." Or the other way around. Or not.

"Dad, you're wrong." A note of small-town-parade triumph in his voice. "Paul wrote eighty-four point five-five percent of the Beatles songs. John wrote seventy-three point six-five percent." Silence. "George wrote twenty-two point one-five percent."

"Poor George. Third place again."

"How do you mean?"

"I just mean that sometimes the other Beatles weren't all that nice to George."

"Why?"

"Age difference, mostly." George was younger than the others, I reminded him, nearly two years younger than John. And George had worshipped John back when the boys were teenagers in Liverpool, even trying to tag along when John went on dates. "Remember, all four of them grew up together, and when that happens, you get caught up in certain roles. No matter how old you get—I bet you'll see this someday with your own sisters—you don't ever forget who's older and who's the baby." Sam had two sisters, ages six and four. "Your roles in your family don't really change over time, even if you've changed. And the Beatles were kind of a family."

Already there were lessons Sam had picked up from the band. Things I could teach him, or my wife, Maggie, could, using the Beatles as real-life characters, stand-ins for guys everywhere.

But in the end, he would teach us more than we could ever teach him: names, dates, working song titles, even the Liverpool bus routes Paul and George took as adolescents. An excellent though reluctant piano student, Sam's ears picked up little things in Beatles songs that my own ears trampled and crushed—a near-imperceptible rattling at the end of "Long, Long, Long," caused, Sam told me, by a half-drunk bottle of wine vibrating atop the Leslie speaker in the Abbey Road studios ("Blue Nun," he clarified); the swirling, geyserlike sound effects in "Yellow Submarine" deriving from John blowing bubbles through a straw while George swished water around in a bucket; the barely audible percussion in "Lovely Rita" caused by the Beatles dragging metal hair combs through sheets of toilet paper; the symphonic crescendo that caps off "A Day in the Life" culminating on the chord of E major. I knew none of these things.

Eventually Sam would roll off the bed, and a few minutes later from his bedroom, I'd hear the opening strains of "Taxman," the genial hook of "We Can Work It Out," or John Lennon's elegantly acid vocal from "A Day in the Life." It was like being sawed awake, and for the umpteenth time since this had all started, I experienced a few tormented moments of self-doubt: This was our fault, wasn't it? And it was OK, right?

"Could you turn that down a bit?" I'd yell, coming into his room to help him mobilize. As he dressed for school, Sam casually explained to me that Paul McCartney had written "Getting Better" during a walk in the park with his sheepdog, Martha, and that John Lennon wrote "I'm So Tired" in India, when he couldn't get to sleep. Oh, and did I know that Father McKenzie from "Eleanor Rigby" was a stranger's last name that Paul swiped from the London phone book (though he composed the song using the working name "Father McCartney"), and that it was Ringo who came up with the line "Darning his socks / in the night"?

It wasn't just Beatles data he knew cold. He was also casually acquainted with the group's sidemen — Billy Preston playing the keyboards on "Get Back," Eric Clapton donating a guitar solo as a favor to George Harrison on "While My Guitar Gently Weeps" — as well as with assorted Beatles' cameo players, girlfriends, wives, and children: the Stu Sutcliffes and Pete Bests, the Cynthias, Yokos, Maureens, Pattis, Lindas, Julians, Stellas, and Heathers. He also knew the solo work each Beatle had put out after the band dissolved, from *Ram* to *All Things Must Pass* to *Sentimental Journey* to *Double Fantasy.*

His third-floor bedroom wasn't an all-American room. It was an all-English room, lacking only a three-pronged outlet and a draft. Fab Four memorabilia rushed at you as the door swung open. A *Beatles '65* LP hung on the near wall next to a faded print of Klaus Voorman's intricate *Revolver* cover. An antique Beatles lunchbox sat hunched on his windowsill. Directly across the room from his bed hung a two-by-three-foot blowup of the zebra-crossing on the *Abbey Road* album cover. Taped to its bottom rim were two dozen or so postcards of the Beatles in various incarnations: nervously endearing in their first suits; martial-looking in *Sgt. Pepper* regalia; seedy-looking and estranged for *The White Album;* and finally, lost in their own bickering thoughts as they jammed on a Savile Row rooftop during an overcast London afternoon in *Let It Be.*

In Sam's dresser drawer sat a Blue Meanies T-shirt and a Beatles-faces necktie; on the room side of his door hung a Beatles calendar he could glance at when he wasn't telling the time with his Yellow Submarine wristwatch; on one of his wall sconces hung a white plastic pendant you see draped on hotel doorknobs, except rather than saying "Do Not Disturb," this one read, "It's Been a Hard Day's Night." Next to his portable CD player sat, scattered and mostly caseless, the scratched CDs of *Help!, A Hard Day's Night, Sgt. Pepper's Lonely Hearts Club Band, The White Album, Please Please Me, Magical Mystery Tour, Abbey Road, Meet the Beatles, Revolver, Rubber Soul,* both volumes of *Past Masters,* the two slightly redundant greatest-hits collections *The Red Album* and *The Blue Album,* the recently rereleased *Yellow Submarine* soundtrack, and a hard-to-find double CD called *The Beatles Live at the BBC.*

Enough already—but there was more. In his bookcase, beside *The Lorax* and a couple of Harry Potter books, sat nearly a half dozen battered paperbacks devoted to Beatles trivia, to Paul-is-dead clues and to the origins of every Beatles song ever recorded, including ones I'd never heard of, like "Youngblood" and "Cry for a Shadow" and "I'm Gonna Sit Right Down and Cry over You." Downstairs, scattered among the videos and DVDs, were his copies of *Help!, A Hard Day's Night, Yellow Submarine, Magical Mystery Tour, The Compleat Beatles,* the eight-volume *Beatles Anthology* (the *Let It Be* video was tied up in litigation, though he'd seen that, too), and a couple of cheap-o, foreign-made knockoffs with titles like *Beatles Bonanza* and *Beatles Uncollected — The Lost Archives.*

Directly over Sam's narrow bed, in a purple frame, hung the pièce de résistance.

I wasn't very enthusiastic when Sam told my wife and me that he wanted to write Paul McCartney a fan letter. "He's probably incredibly overextended," I told him, adding that Paul McCartney was (well, undoubtedly; I couldn't say for sure) a horribly busy person with a global songwriting empire to run, and music to write and record and produce, and grown children to tend to, probably an altogether overly written-to person. Plus, I'd done enough interviews with well-known people to know that most celebrities were less affable than their public images would lead you to believe. "You have to be a bastard to make it and that's a fact," John Lennon said once. "And the Beatles were the biggest bastards on earth."

But mostly, I didn't want Sam to get his feelings hurt when several years went by and he still hadn't gotten an answer. "Paul probably gets truckloads of mail," I explained. My wife made a face at me. I was being a spoilsport.

"I don't care if Paul doesn't write me back," Sam said.

So that night, Maggie and I helped Sam improvise a short, heartfelt letter to Paul McCartney, which included a crayoned drawing of a smiling, left-handed guy holding a guitar. If I were Paul McCartney, I would have liked getting something like this in my mailbox—a note complimenting me on my voice and bass-guitar playing, particularly on *Abbey Road,* and closing with the words, "I love you, Paul." The next day, I mailed off the letter to Paul's London offices, then forgot about it.

School ended; the neighborhood thinned out as neighbors left for vacation; parking places showed up on our street; air conditioners dripped onto sidewalks and gardens. Weeks went past.

I remember the night clearly. We were in the harried first minutes of returning from a week at the beach, the car double-parked outside, our accumulated mail splashed across the dining-room table, when I caught sight of the beige, official-looking envelope addressed to Sam. I noticed that my son's name and address were neatly typed out on a computer label, that there was no return address, and that the envelope bore the faint pink smack of a U.K. postmark.

A few moments later, Sam said, peacefully, happily, "Paul wrote me back."

"Paul who?" I had come up behind Sam now, and I noticed the signature. "Oh, *shit!* I mean—" My wife let out a scream, then clapped her fingers over her mouth. "Oh, my God, I can't believe it," I heard her say through her fingers. Then she screamed again, but without fingers this time.

The letter was typed on a business-size cream-colored

sheet, with "Paul McCartney" preprinted in dark, wiry script across the top. Addressed to "Samuel," and composed in thoughtfully plain language that any child could understand, Paul thanked my son for his words about his singing and bass-guitar playing. He was surprised and also happy, he said, to find out that there were seven-year-olds in the world who knew and liked *Abbey Road*. The letter closed by relaying warm wishes not just to Sam, but to Sam's parents.

The signature was in a dashing, daunting black ink, and beneath the *ney* of *McCartney,* Paul — now indisputably the kindest, finest, greatest, best, most generous, and brilliant Beatle, the group's guts, soul, brains, and heart — had drawn a doodle of a beaming, freckled, round-faced kid, as if to say, *Thanks for your drawing. Here's mine.*

"I told you he'd answer me," Sam kept saying as we all read and reread the letter, putting it down and picking it up countless times. (That night, I slithered into Sam's room where he lay asleep to pore over the letter again, to suck up meanings from its every word, to memorize every loop of Paul's signature. *My best to you and your parents.* Parent. That was me, the parent. *Yessss!*) Ten feet away from me, Sam was enjoying the pure sleep of a boy who lived in a just universe: you write someone a letter; he'll write you back.

About a year and a half earlier, I had started to realize that my son and I were having problems.

The signs were slight but they were accumulating. For the longest time, I hardly noticed them; I was too busy.

Which was, as I think back on it, a large part of the problem.

Though Sam didn't want to hurt my feelings, it was obvious that he preferred spending time with his mother, his babysitter, his two sisters, his friends, the risk-loving kid next door, the Border collie two doors down, anybody but me. Earlier that year, he'd brought home a simple drawing from first-grade art class. Titled "My Family," the picture showed four figures of various sizes, all wide-eyed and genially, generically beaming. There was one problem: there were five people in our family. "So where am I?" I asked with false casualness. "Oh," is the only thing Sam said, his green gaze drifting down to his knees. Then, "I think maybe you're in another one."

I was finding it harder and harder to talk to my seven-year-old. My conversations with him started off fluently enough, then stiffened, froze, and broke off. How was it possible, I wondered over and over again, that I could feel awkward around Sam? Of all people? Seven years earlier, I could remember him bundled up between my wife and me, gorgeous in his infant's moody indignity. He was as compulsively watchable as the Zapruder film.

Looking down into his crib day after day, month after month, I could understand finally one reason why weddings were such tribal events. The families intuited that their features would someday end up mashed together in the faces of future grandchildren. My mother and my wife's father, warmly collusive during our wedding, now met up permanently in Sam's eyebrows; my dad acknowledged me in a friendly glance from his coastal grave; my sister-in-law's bottom lip pursed up in annoyance against my great-grand-mother's top lip. Ancestors on both sides crowded into Sam's face, jostling for placement. Somewhere in that checker-board of features, too, were glimmers of his own future face: a teenager sealed in his room; a college boy hobbling on taped crutches; a new father; a farmer; a chef; a diplomat; a bond salesman; a retired rug merchant; an Oscar winner for Best Animated Short. Whatever made him happy: that was my only ambition for him.

As the first of what would be three children, Sam was our practice baby, the test case. He taught Maggie and me how to be parents. As a reward for his patience, we gave him excessive caution and great food. He ate the expensive Earth's Best brand (his younger sister got Gerber's, and I joked that his youngest got dead mice; the more children you have, the sloppier you get).

But as Sam got older, I seemed to be mummifying before his eyes. I didn't really know what to talk about with him. More often than not, I found myself standing across the room from my son, my posture defensive, my voice thinner and higher than usual. I couldn't tell him "I love you" with-out shuffling around like a hayseed. *He makes you nervous,* I realized during one of those times, with stabbing wonder-ment. The up-close, burrowing-mole carnality of him as a baby now felt dreamt, psychedelically distant. At the ages of seven and forty, my son and I were like two teenagers suffer-ing through a series of jumpy, forgettably inept first dates.

It would begin first thing in the morning. I walked Sam to school past the supermarket and the overflowing trash barrel on the corner. "So," I'd say, "what's on the roster for today?"

He didn't know *roster*. Why did I use words like that around him? "I mean, what's up, what's happening for you at school today?"

He glanced up at me, having absorbed without comment the false note. "I don't know, really. Just . . . the usual."

"Hmmm." Then, as I spied a familiar cyclone of newspapers, candy wrappers, and restaurant menus now spinning before us on the street corner, I'd offer up a winning remark like, "God, look at all this junk." Otherwise our walks were, for the most part, silent, until I kissed him fumblingly on the forehead good-bye, and then he'd run up the steps into school.

Was this how I'd end up lodged in his memory, that arbitrary judge that I knew firsthand could recall the one cloudy day in a week of sunny ones? "Yeah, my dad was like the third ghost in *A Christmas Carol*," the adult Sam would say gloomily to his wife. "The faceless one in the black cape who went around pointing at things."

Instead of hanging out with my family, I worked. When I wasn't locked in my office, I was out looking for work, or traveling on behalf of this or that project, scrambling toward a future so easeful and palm tree–lined it would afford me . . . time with my family.

Was I missed all that terribly? I doubted it. What did fathers do precisely? In my experience, fathers often had a pretty easy time of it. They received abnormal acclaim for seemingly minimal effort—bouncing a kid on their shoulders or remembering to put matching socks on an infant in subzero weather.

At the same time, I could sense fatherlessness when I came across it in other people. It was the vague, yearning quality I saw in some guys whose dads had died young, or who were drunks, or who had otherwise gone missing. It had the force of a craving—blunt, ardent. It was probably no coincidence that John Lennon, who was raised by women and who once said of his childhood, "The men were invisible," was the angriest, most self-destructive of all four Beatles.

Before Sam was born, I gave myself a solemn lecture, filled with clumsy double negatives: *You will never not discuss with your son important topics. You will never not not reveal yourself to him. You will never not have time for him. You will not work too hard, or shut your kids out of your office, or your life.* Then I'd breached each one of these commandments.

Maybe I was simply communing with my own father.

My dad was a schoolmaster, a locally legendary one. An owlish, eccentric, crew-cut, suavely disheveled man who spent nearly four decades teaching English at a New England private school, he was a Bostonian by birth and by temperament, and a paradox: a soulful, conservative man who loved jazz; a former miler addicted to cigarettes; a law-school dropout; a lover of Shakespeare, Tennyson, omelets, good wine, and Alvin and the Chipmunks. Rumors chopped lightly around him—that he was paid a dollar a year, that he'd been a World War II navigator who'd flown twenty-three B-17 missions while most soldiers could manage only three, that is, if they came back at all. Number one wasn't true; number two was, though I only stumbled upon the details a decade after he died. Relatively old when he had my sister and me (forty-two), he frightened me when I was little — he seemed grumpy, self-absorbed, his thoughts someplace else — and though his humor and decency were obvious to all, and our relationship over the years was loving, it was shyer and more formal than I would've liked. Early on, I think he decided, with some relief, that I "got" him, and he "got" me, and that part of what made our connection so first-rate was that neither of us saw the need to make it any more explicit. I took this as the natural order between fathers and boys (it fit perfectly my own shy nature), and so a whole life slipped away between us. Looking back, I was as much to blame as he was. So I grew up with a belief that the most important things in life — what you were feeling, what you believed in — led by silent example. This was, after all, one of the marks of his generation.

These guys saved the world. What else did you want from them?

More. At least I did.

Yet, without thinking about it, I christened my fatherhood by repeating the approach I'd grown up with. It was like blowing a pointless red heart into the sky: *Dad, I'm like you — aren't you proud of me?*

I hadn't the slightest idea who I was as a father. I didn't even want to talk about it. I was jammed in the hinge of two colliding generations, my dad's and my own, adhering to and not liking elements of both.

Then one day, I was leafing through Sam's schoolwork, which the school sent home every month or so. His teacher had asked the class to fill in the answers to five or six mildly probing questions. In response to "What makes you sad?" Sam had written, "When my dad goes away." Two lines beneath that, in answer to "What makes you happy?" he'd written, "Spending time with my dad."

I didn't know what to think, how to react. I was sand-bagged—shocked that my son needed me and unhappy with myself for not seeing more clearly that he did.

That week, I made a full-frontal effort. I would be around more. I would sit still for meals. I would rearrange my schedule. I would work less and spend more time with my kids. On Sunday, I took Sam to the park near our house. No sisters, no dog, just us. From the back, his gait uncannily resembled my father's—long legs, slightly knock-kneed. It wasn't an athlete's walk but the amble of a thoughtful person, absent, more settled in the head than in the body. I couldn't help thinking that, in some ways, I was accompanying my own father to the park, permitting him a bit of run-around fun he'd maybe lacked himself growing up. Or maybe I was taking myself to the park thirty-five years ago. Or maybe I should simply just stop crossing my wires.

I'd brought along a whiffle ball and a plastic bat. Setting up shop near a group of dog walkers, Sam and I threw the fat ball back and forth a few times. "Try and catch it like this, Sam, kind of open-handed," I called out after a few throws. Then, "You want to give it a little twist, too."

Little twist? You mean like Chubby Checker? And wasn't "open-handed" a Buddhist term, not a baseball term? The ball made an ugly clap as it hit Sam's new glove, or the heel of my hand when he overhanded it back at me. It was the hollow sound of the wrong myth at work. No—sports wasn't going to do the trick here. Plus, I cannot tell a lie: I was more interested in introducing my kids to cultural stuff than I was in teaching them how to throw a fastball.

Without being precious about it, I wanted all three of my children to know about the cities of the world. I wanted them to learn at least one language other than English. I wanted them to know about their ancestry, but not be hemmed in by it. I wanted them to be street-smart, charming, and fearless. I wanted them to be kind to other people (they didn't have to *like* them, just be kind to them) and to respect conflicting points of view. I wanted them to be conversant with classical music, to know and appreciate jazz, and to at least give opera a listen. I wanted them to understand music's power, how an old song coming from the radio could freeze you in your tracks and invoke all the complexity of the past—a love affair, a long-gone friend, the walls of an old bedroom, a time you thought you knew yourself well. Could books or movies do that? Not really. And I wanted them to have standards, for them to know "good" and "great" on those rare occasions they came across it, as I was determined they would.

• • •

At seven, nearly eight years old, Sam was tall for his age, and slender. *Beautiful* was a word a lot of people used about his face; *soulful* was one they used to describe his personality. He was green-eyed, shaggy-haired, slightly absent. There was a tenderness about him, as well as a note of caution. It was as though he'd found out already that the world was rigged, and you had to be careful where you stepped and who with, too. He was soft-spoken, but meticulous with words. Sometimes he got snagged in details, and you had to hustle him along. He could also be comically oblivious, the sort of boy who puts his sweatpants on backward, or who Velcros his right sneaker onto the left foot. His vagueness blurred his edges, made him appear groggy sometimes. But it had its reasons. He was touched by things, and I think he'd fashioned a bumper, or a buttress, around himself to lower his chances of getting slammed around.

But this cloudy quality concealed a punctilious mind. In his most seemingly out-of-it moods, Sam took in every-thing anybody said and was able to repeat it back as if read-ing from a page. Once when he and I were sorting through the toy chest in his room, I was amazed to find he could identify nearly a hundred obscure, snapped-off or mangled toy pieces. A fragment of gray plastic? The broken sword tip from an action figure a friend gave him for his fifth birth-day. An inch-long loop of string? From the broken green yo-yo his cousin had given him three years earlier. A tiny green plastic cone? Why, from the Clue game, of course.

When I read aloud to him before bed, I'd gotten into the bad habit of paraphrasing for the sake of expedience. But he caught me every time. "'Yes, Rusty said,'" I would drone, "'I want to go into the—'"

Sam would break in: "'Yes, Rusty *exclaimed*.'"

"'Yes, Rusty exclaimed. 'Stop it, stop it!' Cora said. Then Daisy—'"

"'Stop it, stop it, Cora *ejaculated, tooting her shiny red horn.*'"

"OK! '*Stop it, stop it, Cora ejaculated, tooting her shiny red—*'"

Nowhere was this weird precision more apparent than when he dug into a topic, or an object, that interested him. On his third birthday, he ignored the pile of presents in front of him, fixating instead on the fat blue train-shaped candle atop his birthday cake. Two weeks later, he was still playing with the train candle, attempting to stuff it inside one of his Brio tunnels. Other minor and major obsessions followed, some generically boyish (cars, trucks, trains, backhoes, dinosaurs), some odder: the Alamo, the *Odyssey*, Dame Edna Everage.

Obsessions seemed to keep him balanced. They gave him lift, focus, direction. Just before discovering the Beatles, he was preoccupied with the *Titanic*. He saw James Cameron's film so many times he could recite the dialogue along with the doomed lovers. I bought him books, posters, a foot-long inflatable *Titanic* to play with in the tub. I was surprised when I found his attention riveted less on the chaos and violence of the sinking ship than on the sadness of it all—the gallantry of some of the men, the mother telling her little son that things were going to be all right, the shipboard musicians launching into another chorus as the liner went down.

Then, Sam just lost interest one day. The blowup *Titanic* slumped in the basket next to the bathtub, along with the broken shark, the stumpy triceratops, and his sisters' tea set. Over the next few weeks, Sam idled around the house like a hobo. He lazed on the couch, staring at nothing. He timed himself holding his breath. He got into stupid fights with his sisters. He would appear suddenly in the kitchen, a stormy look in his eyes, then smile sheepishly, explaining that he'd forgotten why he was there. He seemed to be searching for a peg on which he could hang the rest of his life. In the meantime, he lived out his seven-year-old's life — school, friends, skating, roller-blading, bike riding, pizza eating, followed by summer, then camp — but something was missing.

"He needs a new obsession," Maggie remarked one night, "ASAP."

For the past year, my wife and I had been looking for an alternative to children's music. Unfortunately, we weren't having any luck, and our family had splintered into stubborn, highly opinionated musical camps. Maggie liked listening to the news, Motown, and classical music. I liked pre-1965 jazz, requiems, and call-in psychology shows. The two girls were partial to music from the *Madeline* cartoons and soundtracks of Disney movies that featured gutsy, scantily clad heroines. Sam's taste in music was more scattered and quirky, and he tended to welcome repeated hearings of the same song—Enya's "Sail Away," for example, or Roger Miller's "King of the Road."

All three children seemed to enjoy a mild-mannered Canadian singer named Raffi; a group of kinetic musicians called Rosenshontz; and the Sugar Beats, who mostly sang knockoff covers of old Motown hits.

It wasn't that this music was terrible, because it wasn't. It was just that after the four hundredth or so listen, your ears began to revolt against the republic of childhood. You just couldn't face hearing another song about a baby bat, or a peanut butter sandwich, or an oat. Three little cats. Five little frogs. Six little ducks. These kid-friendly melodies stuck in your head and swam relentless laps there. I'd begun to fall asleep at night humming "Joshua Giraffe" and "Robin in the Rain" and "Spider on the Floor," forgetting that once, I'd thrashed around in the sixteenth row of a Clash concert, and had beer sprayed on me at CBGB's. Or was that somebody else?

Around this time, I noticed the first streaks of popular culture penetrating my kids' lives. Groups that were more brands than bands. One-hit phenomena. I loved a few things I was hearing (the Spice Girls, Eminem, the Yeah Yeah Yeahs), but overall the musical landscape felt empty, and worse, ephemeral. To paraphrase an old Woody Allen joke, the food was terrible and there were no second helpings either. This junk was the soundtrack to their childhood? What about talent? What about music that lasted? What about songs that were *about* something? Or even deliberately *not* about something? In short, I reacted in the same way my own parents must have greeted the music I dragged home thirty years ago.

Then it hit both of us: Why not introduce the kids to the Beatles?

As the Beatles' breakup neared, John Lennon complained that the band offered something for everyone. Even "grannies" liked them, he said, the implication being that he'd disgraced himself as a rock 'n' roller. He might have been just as unhappy that today the Beatles appeal so viscerally to children, but it's a fact, maybe even a phenomenon. In spite of Lennon's efforts, nearly a half-century has defanged the group, reducing its innovations and iconoclasms to something warmer and fuzzier. By the time Sam stumbled onto the band, a small industry had arisen, shrewdly linking the interests of thirty-something parents with children in CDs like *Baby Road,* and offering up the notion that you could rear kids as hip and knowing as, well, *you.* Other CDs for kids repositioned certain Beatles songs as easily digestible sermons for the very young: "With a Little Help from My Friends" (buddies are important), "Here Comes the Sun" (hey, it's not so bad), and "Mother Nature's Son" (being outside is healthy). What's more, "Octopus's Garden," "All Together Now," and "Yellow Submarine" are, at heart, children's anthems.

Marketing aside, the Beatles' universe offers up the dreamy self-containment of any great magical realm. The songs are laden with animals (piggies, bulldogs, kittens, walruses, birds, blue jays), cartoonlike characters (Bungalow Bill, Rocky Raccoon, the Sun King, Polythene Pam, the Eggman), and blazing images (strawberry fields, tangerine skies, glass onions, poppies on a tray). The Beatles' lives weren't at odds with these images but extensions of them. What's more, the band gave off a spotless, infectious energy, a *cleanliness* that satisfied but didn't overwhelm Sam's growing appetite for grownup music and older-guy role models.

The Beatles were cool. Good-looking. Confident. They never seemed to be posturing. They weren't ashamed to smile. They weren't harsh or boorish. They were witty, goofy sometimes. The songs and the instruments were bracing and exotic — sitars, Mellotrons, piccolo trumpets, Indian table harps, a forty-one-piece symphony orchestra — and they also offered great variety: if you didn't like one cut, chances were good you'd like the next. Thanks in part to their carefully idealizing early films, each Beatle came across as recognizably distinct and shaded in with the broad strokes of fairytale characters.

Plus, how do you define *charm*? Narrowly speaking, it is the ineffable capacity to be unselfishly pleasing. If you're charmed by someone, you're put at your ease. The Beatles' version of charm — a capacity to be rebellious without being rude, smart-assed but in a way that made you root for them — came across from their first press conference.

Still, in the end, what happened to Sam had more to do with Beatles music than anything else. Forty years later, it was jolting, familiar, and, at the same time, exceedingly strange. It could still give you goose bumps. Unusual among rock songs, you could make out every single lyric.

Sam found the melodies easy to memorize. Over time, I would recast the decision to introduce the Beatles to the kids as more personal and complicated than simply finding music all five of us could bear listening to inside a car. The Beatles gave us a sidelong means of telling the children about the people we were, or thought we were, once.

Sam found out about the Beatles at the start of a three-day holiday weekend.

We — all five of us — were halfway through a six-hour car trip, racing along a crowded interstate in central New England. Sam had the far back seat all to himself. Attempting to stretch out while staying secure under his seatbelt, he'd reached a tortured compromise: the reclining slouch. With both hands, he fiddled and jabbed at the Color Gameboy I'd given him for his seventh birthday, which we allowed him to play, with some ambivalence, half an hour a day.

Somewhere in the middle of Connecticut, by prior arrangement, Maggie removed the cassette of *Abbey Road* from her purse and slid it into the car's tape player.

The cruel, muffled voice of John Lennon murmuring, "*Shoot me,*" the *me* snapped off again and again by the guitar thrust, shuddered out the car speakers.

From "Come Together" to "Her Majesty" — and in between, "Something," "Maxwell's Silver Hammer," "Oh! Darling," "Octopus's Garden," "I Want You (She's So Heavy)," "Here Comes the Sun," "Because," "You Never Give Me Your Money," "Sun King," "Mean Mr. Mustard,"

"Polythene Pam," "She Came in through the Bathroom Window," "Golden Slumbers," "Carry That Weight," and "The End" — *Abbey Road*, followed immediately by *Rubber Soul*, followed by an encore of *Abbey Road*, serenaded us through three states.

That might have been the beginning and the end of Sam's experience with the Beatles. It wouldn't have been the first time that a rock group had failed to make a good impression. On another car trip, I'd put on the Rolling Stones' *Hot Rocks*, and Sam's only response after a few minutes was to ask me if I wouldn't mind turning it down. The same went for the Patti Smith, Blondie, UB40, Bob Dylan, The Band, and Steely Dan. Paul Simon was OK, though Sam complained that most of his songs sounded the same. Sam's sisters had a soft spot for Sam Cooke, Annie Lennox, Marvin Gaye, and Sting. All three of them liked Stevie Wonder, James Taylor, Bob Marley, and the song "Moondance," but could take or leave everything else Van Morrison ever recorded.

This time around, the car was silent. No one crying, or complaining, or squabbling. No requests for juice boxes, or water, or grapes, or apples, or Doritos, or Reese's Peanut Butter Cups, or bathrooms, or crayons. The back seat was as still as a valley in midsummer.

In the rush to unpack and get resettled in a new house, I forgot about the Beatles. It wasn't until after dinner that I noticed Sam was gripping the *Abbey Road* cassette. I wasn't sure how long he'd had it, but when he handed it to me, the plastic was warm and thumbed. "Dad," he said in his serious way, "is it OK for me to bring this in the house?" When I told him of course it was (well, in part because it already *was* inside the house), he hesitated before asking me whether it was OK for him to play it in his Walkman.

Later that night, I made my way into the bedroom, where Sam lay surrounded by pillows, drinking hot chocolate. "Dad?" he said in an urgent, stuffed-up voice (he had a cold), "You know when you hear a song and then you can't stop thinking about it? Even when you *try* to stop thinking about it?"

He was known in our family for non sequiturs, and for abruptly resuming conversations that had taken place hours, days, even months earlier. When he was six, we drove through Pennsylvania Dutch country. A year later, when I asked if he wanted to go on an errand with me, he hesitated, then told me he didn't want to ride in a car because, "I prefer the ways of the Amish." Another time, Maggie sat him down to go over her family tree, which included a distant kinship with Abraham Lincoln. Six months later, in the middle of his bath, Sam cried out suddenly, "I cannot *believe* someone would shoot my poor cousin through the eyeball!"

"Sure, I get songs stuck in my head all the time," I said now.

"It's the one that goes . . ." and Sam sang the first few bars of "Octopus's Garden."

I couldn't help feeling a funny pleasure, a weirdly entrepreneurial pride. The Beatles seemed mine, suddenly, a gorgeous thing I could pull out from under my coat. "Ringo Starr wrote that song," I said, "with a little assistance from the others," adding helpfully that Ringo was the Beatles' drummer.

Were the Beatles alive, my son wanted to know?

Three out of four of them were, I explained, adding that a crazy fan killed John in front of his apartment building in 1980, in New York City. "He was my age when he died," I went on; then, not wanting to imply that all forty-year-olds were in danger of dying, I added that this was a very rare occurrence.

Sam seemed confused. "So were there three Beatles or four Beatles?"

"Four," and I named them.

Sam mulled over the last one. "That's not his real name?"

"Ringo? Actually, it was Richard. Richard Starkey. But he wore a lot of rings when he was younger. So everybody called him 'Ringo.'"

When Sam proceeded to quiz me about each individual Beatle, I didn't quite know where to begin. It was like trying to describe string or grass or the walls, deceptively commonplace objects you realized you didn't know at all. Later, Maggie would remind me how starved we were for Beatles news when we were younger, compared to what we know now. How elusive the group was, the little we knew about them communicated via dark hints, rumors, clues, and press releases. The band's mystery was symbolized by the shadowy apple in the center of their LPs, a totem Sam would one day inform me was inspired by *Le Jeu de Mourre* by René Magritte, an artist whose work Paul collected. (Over the course of their marriage, Linda McCartney bought and presented Paul with Magritte's easel and his eyeglasses. At least that's what Sam told me.)

But a few minutes later, drawing on my murky recollection of legend, hearsay, liner notes, magazine articles, Internet ramblings, and books I'd skimmed over the years, I managed to piece together a brief bio of each Beatle.

John Lennon. Middle name Winston, a nod to then prime minister Churchill. Born, as the rest of the Beatles were, in a northern English port city called Liverpool. "The Liverpool accent was quite distinct," I said. "Very nasal. A lot of people believe it was caused by pollution." John was the Beatles' leader, I went on, and the others looked up to him. He was a piece of work, sharp, bright, belligerent, sarcastic, the author of several books—"Do you know how unusual it is?" I broke in, "for a rock 'n' roll guy to write books?"—and along with Paul McCartney, the cowriter of most of the Beatles' songs. Following his divorce from a local girl named Cynthia, who bore him a son, Julian, John remarried a Japanese artist and musician named Yoko Ono. They had one son, Sean, and lived in New York until his death.

"I was petrified of John Lennon back when I was your age," I added.

"Why?"

"I guess I thought there was something a little scary about his face and his voice. That he was probably not very nice in person." I shrugged. "It might have had something to do with his little glasses."

Paul McCartney. The most affable, amiable, adorable Beatle. Versatile. Eager to please. A tendency to be controlling. The Beatle who effectively took over the group in the late sixties. Some critics unfairly considered Paul Winnie-the-Pooh to John's Eeyore. "A lot of people thought of Paul as the happy-go-lucky Beatle and John as the darker, more tortured one," I said to Sam. A famous example of this came from a song called "Getting Better," I went on, when Paul sang (and wrote) "It's getting better all the time," while John contributed the chorus, "It can't get no worse."

"Mom has kind of a crush on Paul," I said, "and on Linda. I'm sure she'll tell you about it someday."

George Harrison. The youngest Beatle. The son of a bus driver. Known by many as the "quiet" Beatle (a tag loudly disputed by friends and family members after his death). Questing. Mystical. Perennially dissatisfied. Could be a little pedantic. It was George who introduced the others to Indian music and Eastern philosophy. "When I say the others," I told Sam, "I don't just mean the other three Beatles. I mean the rest of the world, too." Of all the Beatles, George enjoyed the most critically acclaimed solo career after the breakup. "Paul and John didn't really take George all that seriously as a musician during the Beatles years. I don't think it was easy for George, being the youngest and being overshadowed all the time."

Ringo Starr. The Beatles' drummer. The oldest of the four. Supremely likable, the most natural actor of the four, a comic foil for the other three. To this day, never taken en-

tirely seriously by Beatles fans or critics and unjustly considered, along with George, more fortunate than fated. Still,
with his sexy/homely, underdog appearance, Ringo quickly
became America's favorite Beatle when the band came here
in the early 1960s. Not much of a songwriter (as Ringo was
the first to admit) but a chummy, distinctively flat-voiced
singer.

"So that's it," I said. "Four guys. Four friends." John and
Paul, then teenagers, met at a Liverpool church fete (a *fete*
being a kind of village social occasion, typically held on
weekends, on church grounds, I explained) where John was
performing with his band, the Quarry Men. Impressed and
maybe a little alarmed by Paul's musicianship, John invited
him to join the group. Eventually, George Harrison, whom
Paul knew from riding the bus every morning, came
aboard, along with a local drummer, Pete Best, and a gui-
tarist, Stuart Sutcliffe. Following the Beatles' musical apprenticeship in Germany, Paul nudged Sutcliffe out of the
group and Best was later replaced by Ringo.

The Beatles were together for less than a decade, released
approximately two hundred songs, and broke up in 1970.

"How do you mean that they broke up?"

"They decided to stop being the Beatles. To do other
things with their lives. To get married, have kids, stuff like
that."

Something was happening in Sam's brain. I had the impression of liquid dissolving into earth, roots jolting upward. "But *why?*" he asked, his voice muted. "*Why* did they
have to break up?"

"Lots of different reasons. They weren't getting along.

They weren't really sure what to do next. Both John and Paul had fallen in love—"

Things were getting complicated here, but to my relief, Sam broke in with another question: Why did the group call itself "the Beatles"?

At the time he asked, I had no idea, though eventually I'd come across a few theories. John Lennon loved puns, and obviously, "beat" swiveled nicely into "beatle." Another theory attributed the name to John's love of the beat poetry movement, pervasive in the mid 1950s. Later, Ringo would recall that "beetles" was a slang expression for motorcycle chicks, popularized, and maybe even coined, in the 1954 Marlon Brando biker movie, *The Wild One.* The one thing band members and historians tended to agree on was that John was a huge admirer of Buddy Holly and the Crickets and sought a similar tag for his own band, one preferably involving insects.

Earlier that afternoon, at the kids' request, I'd overturned one of the half dozen logs that enclose the driveway. It was one of our first-day rituals. They liked watching the bugs scatter, the centipedes scare off, the potato bugs play dead. It didn't occur to me that when Sam asked about the band's name, he probably had a vivid image in his head: black, helmet-backed June bugs, thwapping against the screens or buzzing on their backs. He didn't, I realized, even know what the Beatles looked like.

2.
Rubber
Soul

T HE FIRST RECORD ALBUM I ever bought—
in retrospect, I realize I was right around
Sam's age—was the Beatles' *Rubber Soul.*

I can still remember the album propped up against my knees, the cover as familiar to me as my own face, the landscape of hazy green and brown leather, the four faces slightly out of focus, with only one Beatle, John, looking directly and critically at the camera. All four of them were everything I wasn't: cool, rich, popular, famous, longhaired, and grownup.

Over the next six months, I played *Rubber Soul* continuously, the order of the songs taking on a suitelike logic, so quickly internalized it even altered my sense of anticipation. Religiously, and with no cheating permitted, I went all the way through: "Drive My Car," followed by "Norwegian

Wood," followed by "You Won't See Me," followed by "No-where Man," all the way until the final cut, "Run for Your Life," the one cut on the album I didn't much like, but nonetheless kept playing, if only for the pinch of confused fear it gave me every time the lyrics warned the girl (was she a first grader, like me?) that if she didn't pull herself together and do precisely what the Beatles wanted, whatever that was, then that would be "the end" of "little girl."

Back then I must have understood that I wasn't exactly the group's core audience. Also, that there was something illicitly thrilling about the fact that I, a seven-year-old, was listening to the Beatles in the first place. Beatles music was aimed more at people closer to the band members' own age, a group much more immersed in the times at hand (war, drugs, rebellion) than I was in my New England suburb.

For a kid, owning an album had its grandiose pleasures. Your name, or initials, penciled or black-inked on the sleeve or, if you were feeling particularly possessive, on the label in the center of the record itself. That childish clamp: *mine*. Another small step to adulthood was having a favorite song. Mine was "Day Tripper," whose bass line summed up the kind of reckless person I hoped other people might mistake me for, but never did. My older sister had a favorite song, too: "You Don't See Me." Our choices drove no discernible wedge between us. They just sat there, harmless, baffling. Welcome to *taste*, that mysterious thing. Knowing that the songs we liked diverged, I remember studying her, wondering what she heard in that song that I didn't, or couldn't. Music, it seemed, offered important data about other people. It linked you to your siblings. Albums got claimed, passed down, fought over, taped, lost, and scratched (during fights, even deliberately). It wasn't just brothers and sisters, either. Later, when I'd be getting to know a girl, or a male friend, there was inevitably a point when they would press their favorites on you: Joni Mitchell. The Pogues. Elvis Costello. Sonic Youth. The *Black Orpheus* soundtrack. If you didn't like what they liked, something changed. The smallest gulf opened up between you. You were pushing a piece of them away, rejecting information about them that they were offering. Or just maybe you didn't know good music when you heard it.

As a child and later teenager, music played in our house all day and night, often duelingly. Upstairs was the Beatles. In the kitchen an opera may have blared from the radio. And downstairs was the dominant soundtrack of my growing up, my father's jazz, the "good stuff," he called it—Ray Noble, Al Bowlly, Sidney Bechet, Cootie Williams, Johnny Hodges, Duke Ellington, Count Basie, Teddy Wilson, Jelly Roll Morton, Benny Goodman, and so on. I loved that music (to me, it's still the aural equivalent of comfort food), but I couldn't understand or appreciate it the same way my father did. In the same songs, we heard different things. That music came out of a black-and-white world of Churchill, apprehension, patriotism, and train-station kissing; and I was a pampered product of the world of cheese popcorn, *The Partridge Family*, and Watergate. Occasionally, after an evening of wine, my father felt moved to pick up his old, black clarinet, tongue the reed to the right degree of wetness, and play along, squawkingly and with obvious pleasure, to an old Goodman or Ellington tune: "Don't Be That Way" or "If Dreams Come True" or "I Let a Song Go out of My Heart." His rustiness with the instrument seemed more a source of bemusement to him than frustration or irritation. Alone in the living room with his glass of wine close by, heated by the fire's embers, he seemed to me a solitary, tranquil figure.

To this day, I wonder what was going through his mind. What years did that music remind him of? Were his memories specific, hazy, rewarding, upsetting? If music was coded communication, what was he trying to tell our house, or even provoke inside himself? On a few occasions, he'd materialize like a sudden fog in the doorway of the room where I happened to be sitting, the music coloring the house like a threadbare blanket. The graceful emcee's gesture he made, the fingers of one hand curling slightly, announced only: *This is just so you know what perfect sounds like.*

The Beatles always interested him, though I suspect more intellectually, or as a phenomenon, than musically. "Yeah, yeah, yeah," he'd murmur in imitation of their early songs (later, I would find out that Paul McCartney's own father implored his musical son to at least consider "Yes, Yes, Yes"). Still, as the years passed and I brought new LPs home, my father would actually request specific Beatles songs, mostly the jauntier, more vaudevillian tunes Paul had composed in honor of his own father's love of swing. Songs like "Honey Pie," "When I'm Sixty-Four," and "All Together Now."

He also liked "Yellow Submarine," "Your Mother Should Know," "Eleanor Rigby," "Her Majesty," "Good Night," and the lyrics and piano in "Lady Madonna." He was impressed, and a little taken aback, by the French piccolo trumpet solo in "Penny Lane." The tightness, sophistication, and occasional beauty of the Beatles' harmonies took him, I think, by surprise.

He liked the literate lyrics and the cutting world-weariness of John Lennon's voice in "Being for the Benefit of Mr. Kite." Ringo's affably lame voice on "With a Little Help from My Friends." The "Woke up / Got out of bed" snippet from "A Day in the Life." The "-tah" of "bet-tah" in "Getting Better," the "silently" that came before "closing the bedroom door" in "She's Leaving Home," a song that seemed in general to amuse him, particularly the parents' dreary chorus.

The Beatles' Britishisms sat well with him, too. During his time as an air force navigator mostly stationed at an RAF base outside of London, he came to love the English. The Beatles, after all, made reference to Bishop's Gate; the Isle of Wight; and Blackburn, Lancashire. They said *dear* for expensive and *roundabout* for rotary; their lyrics mentioned the opposition leader Edward Heath, the queen, the House of Lords, and the Albert Hall. How many other rock 'n' roll bands did that?

"They're good," he remarked once about the Beatles, "aren't they."

His words thrilled me. This was praise as high as it got. I was desperate for him to like the group. It was an indirect way for him to get to know me, wasn't it? Whenever he came into the room to listen, I was ecstatic. For once, there were things I could teach *him,* using the Beatles as my mouthpieces. I studied his eyes, his brows, his lips, the bow of his head for the tiniest reaction. I'd even go so far sometimes as to ready the needle to fall onto a track I was certain he'd like at the precise moment he came into the room.

"That guy in the blue jacket is Paul," I said to Sam the next morning, "and that's George in the red hat, John in the yellow, and Ringo's the guy holding the trumpet."

I'd spent every summer of my life until the age of eighteen in this house. Over the years, I'd stashed the refuse of my adolescence in the attic, and after breakfast, I coaxed Sam up the old wood ladder with me. He knelt obediently beside me, studying the battered album cover of *Sgt. Pepper's Lonely Hearts Club Band,* which I'd dug out of an old wine crate, along with the LPs of *Magical Mystery Tour, Rubber Soul,* and *A Hard Day's Night.*

"Dad, I think I know that guy," Sam said suddenly.

"Who?"

He was pointing at Ringo. "He's the train conductor."

"I don't think so," I said after a moment. "That's Ringo Starr. You know, the drummer I told you about?"

"Well, Dad, whatever. He plays the train conductor on 'Thomas,' too." A solemn silence. "Except he has a beard now."

We were both right. I'd forgotten. Up until a year ago,

Thomas the Tank Engine was one of Sam's favorite TV shows. Sam looked pleased; he could claim Ringo as his property, too.

"Who are all these other people behind them?" Sam went on.

"Those are just famous people," I explained. "Actors, singers, writers. There's Shirley Temple; she was a child actress. There's Carl Jung; he was a Swiss psychiatrist. Bob Dylan, he's a singer and a songwriter. Oscar Wilde was a playwright . . ."

"You have tons of old records up here," Sam said, gesturing at nearly a dozen slack boxes of opera, classical, jazz, reggae, rock, folk, heavy metal, even the occasional comedy album.

"Tell me about it," I said.

Like most people I knew, I was at a loss to know what to do with my LPs. I never played them anymore. I never looked at them. I never talked about them. My own pointless loyalty to them annoyed me. But what should I do with them — toss them out? Give them away? Sell them? I couldn't. I loved them, or at least I had once — and I felt sorry for them now, their shiny licorice sides now looking as outdated as actors in blackface.

I browsed through carton after carton. Some thirty years after I'd misplaced it, or had it nicked, I was still halfheartedly looking for the Beatles' *Yesterday and Today.* The cover showed the Beatles perched glumly atop and inside an oversized packing trunk. But this trunk shot was, in fact, a last-minute replacement for Robert Whitaker's original photo, known cheerfully by Beatles aficionados as the "Butcher Cover." This one showed them clad in blood-soaked smocks, dandling decapitated doll bodies, doll heads, and slabs of raw meat on their knees. All four Beatles looked extremely festive. The powers that be at Capitol Records took one look at the butcher photo and refused to release it, hastily plastering the "Trunk Cover" over many of the approximately seven hundred fifty thousand original albums already printed. If you owned a copy of *Yesterday and Today* and knew what you were doing, you could steam off the Trunk Cover in the hopes of finding a genuine Butcher Cover underneath (later, I would discover that a Downey, California, art gallery specializes in "professional Butcher Peeling"). Why go through all the trouble? Money. A collector once bought an unopened, stereo, first-state Butcher Cover album in pristine condition for $25,000.

There was no sign of *Yesterday and Today* in any of the boxes, but I was happy to find my old copy of *Sgt. Pepper,* plus *Rubber Soul, The White Album,* and *Magical Mystery Tour* (with the original booklet, no less!).

Sam was staring down at the cover of *Rubber Soul.* "You scared my poor dad," he said to John reprovingly.

"Hey, don't worry about it, Sam," I said with a little laugh. "I was scared of a whole bunch of things back then."

He wasn't listening. "You scared my poor dad," he repeated, and then I saw his index finger knuckle hovering over John's face, the tip poised to clip him in the mouth. "*Don't* do that."

• • •

Abbey Road had made a dent. After lunch I overheard coming from Sam's bedroom the drum spray of "Come Together," the mournful a cappella "Because," Ringo's drum solo from "The End," the snippet that is "Her Majesty" — and then the tape would start all over again. That afternoon, on the way to the beach, Sam piped up from the back seat, "Can we put on the Beatles again?" before remembering he'd absconded with the tape.

"What's this song about?" he asked me later that day. He'd called me into his bedroom to listen to "Maxwell's Silver Hammer."

"It's about a guy named Maxwell who goes around killing people with a hammer." Facts were facts.

"Oh." Sam's one-note laugh was slightly anxious. "That's not very nice. It's just the melody is so different. And then you realize what the song's actually about . . ."

"Exactly."

"Dad," Sam said. He turned down the volume of his tape recorder. There was an urgency to his stuffed-up voice, and now he confessed, sorrowfully, "I don't really like John all that much, either. His glasses *do* make him look mean."

There was a silence, broken only by the faint, thumping bass line of "Oh! Darling." I wasn't sure what to say. Maybe Sam had picked up the same obscure, edgy unpleasantness that I found in John when I was a kid and had taken it upon himself to shield me — or rather, the me of thirty-five years earlier. More probably, he was telling me we had something in common. It seemed that just as I would discover in the Beatles a means to connect with my son, Sam found in them a way to connect with me.

It wasn't until early that evening that I realized the extent to which the Beatles had made an impression on him.

The house where we were staying looks over a marsh and, beyond it, a sandy beach and a bay that you reach via a series of narrow, waterlogged wooden planks. The kids were allowed to go down to the beach by themselves provided they stayed away from the water and kept themselves visible at all times. Typically, they roamed around in the tall grass and in low tide wandered out onto the bad-smelling mud in search of minnows and shells. But later that night, when I went out onto the porch for one of my periodic child checks, I couldn't believe what I saw.

Sam was standing on one of the soaked planks, his arms and legs frozen in mid stride. In front of him, his two little sisters were doing the same. Or at least, Sam was trying to force them to. His aggrieved voice carried through the marsh. "You're supposed to go *there*, Lily, in *front* of me," he was saying to his sister. She resisted; she wanted to stand behind him. "But you're *Ringo*," Sam went on querulously, adding that, since he was Paul, he should go third; Susannah, the youngest, was supposed to be George. Then I got it: they were re-creating the *Abbey Road* album cover. I made my way down to the beach, and signaled at them across the marsh. "Dad, we're trying to do *Abbey Road*," Sam hollered, "but Lily says *she* wants to be Paul. *I'm* Paul."

"Who's John?" I hollered back.

"*No one.* We're just doing Paul, George, and Ringo."

"Can *I* be Paul?" I asked. It put an end to the argument immediately. "Dad's going to be Paul," Sam announced to his sisters. Which is how I found myself strolling barefoot along a soaked board, back and forth, for the next twenty minutes.

It seemed only natural for Maggie to rent the Beatles' first movie that night.

A Hard Day's Night is a glib, fast-paced black-and-white film, as jumpily cut as anything produced today. At times, everybody in it seems to be talking very loudly at the same time, and the copy we rented from the video store had clearly been around the block a few times. But Sam, perched on the edge of the couch, with a bowl of coffee ice cream on his knees, seemed riveted, particularly by the crush of female fans in the first few scenes. It was among the first few times Sam had seen adults losing control. "Why are they crying?" he asked.

It was tricky to explain. "Those girls love the Beatles," I said, "and they can't believe how close they are to them. Sometimes you can desire something or someone so much it makes you cry. At the same time, I think those girls probably know the odds are long that they'll ever get any closer."

"I would *hate* that," Sam said as a bloc of screaming girls chased the band into a train station.

"The movie treats it as kind of fun," I said, "but this was the Beatles' *life*. Imagine getting mobbed at every single stop. George in particular looks like he's having a blast, but he actually grew to hate being a Beatle."

By midway through the movie, Sam's questions nearly

drowned out the dialogue. "Why does Paul hold his guitar with the neck pointed that way?" he asked.

"He's a lefty," I said.

"Why doesn't Ringo sing any songs in this movie?"

"Ringo didn't have that great a singing voice," I said. "I mean, I happen to love the way Ringo sounds, but—"

"Dad . . ." and Sam was off to the next question, namely, "Are the Beatles really singing, or are they just mouthing the words?" (He'd noticed that the synchronization between song and mouth was a little off.)

Throughout the movie, Sam shot glances over at Maggie, some furtive, sideways; others pleased, others bewildered. He'd never, I don't think, seen a look like that in her eyes before. It intrigued him. Who was this woman who knew every word to every song? Yes, she was his mom, but who was she really? For ninety minutes or so, he was being afforded a glimpse of her without him. At one point, his fingers touched her wrist—just checking in.

If anything, Maggie was even more a Beatles fan than I was. She spent her first twelve years in Europe but came back to the States when her parents divorced in 1970. At almost the same time, the Beatles broke up, ten years together dissolving into acrimony and legal backbiting. Their spiky final release, *Let It Be,* drifted out into the market, preempted by Paul's first solo album, *McCartney,* whose back cover showed a picture of Paul, beaming, bearded, rattily attired, and clutching his new baby daughter, Mary. It was a tender, zany, indelible image. It made the idea of launching a family seem hip and sexy: the idea that you can produce a small accomplice, a third musketeer, whom you and your wife can take with you on your travels.

At the same time, it was, I remember, an anguishing, excluding image. A pact Paul had never signed off on had been broken. He didn't need us anymore, and maybe he never had. Married a year earlier, he gave off an air of sated bliss, and had as well the relieved, free-and-easy look of a bachelor, which, in musical terms, he was now.

Not surprisingly, the two divorces — her parents' and the Beatles' — were forever muddied in Maggie's mind. The black-bordered *Let It Be* and *McCartney* were like minor memorials: the end of a group, the end of a marriage. The homemade-sounding songs of each offered a ragged consolation. If her parents' marriage was partly a victim of cultural changes in the air, in particular early-1970s feminism, my wife found comfort, and a mock Big Sister, in Linda McCartney, who seemed able to deftly combine motherhood, marriage, career, and having fun.

As *A Hard Day's Night* bounded along, I was also glancing at Maggie's eyes. They were the eyes of a girl, a single woman. They revealed an inner life far removed from kitchen counters, kids' demands, or living rooms strewn with toys. Like Sam, I was watching someone who existed independently of me and who, just like me, had gazed down at countless album covers in faraway rooms. As a guy observing a woman observing the Beatles, my understanding, I knew, was limited. But there's a point in the movie when Paul and George are standing before a single mike. Their voices are joined, their faces nearly touching. They look fresh, improbably young. In that second, I caught, at least I thought I did, a flash of what my wife was responding to: *boys*. Sexy boys with guitars.

The house has a cavernous living room with very little furniture in it, a space nearly ideal for dancing. And after the movie ended, and the girls were done with their baths, Maggie put on the *Hard Day's Night* soundtrack and blasted it.

Stretching out on the couch, I watched as Sam's two sisters streamed around their mother, grabbing her knees, vying for her hands. Knowing only that this new music somehow turned her on, they competed for her attention: who'd get to dance with her first? Pick *me* up, the smaller one kept imploring, but my wife, who'd been with the kids all day, wanted a little time by herself. Now it was her older sister's turn. She wanted to be spun around, but Maggie waved her off, too. Tears: both girls wanted *her*. Pausing long enough to skip over "If I Fell" to "Can't Buy Me Love," Maggie surrendered to the fact that kids were omnivores. They would eat you if they could. And so all three of the girls began dancing.

They were a transfixing sight. They were liquid, ecstatic. They had no fight with their bodies. They just adored being girls. They made you wish the word hadn't been turned into a minor insult. Sam, though, was pressed up against a bookcase, gazing mutely at the three of them.

Now, Maggie tried to coax him over to dance to "Any Time at All." Sam shook his head hard, twice. I could tell he wanted to dance, but he was feeling shy. "*Please?*" she begged.

Finally, it occurred to him: a way to submit and sit it out at the same time. Taking Maggie's hand, he came forward eagerly. For a second, he appeared to be on the verge of joining in, but instead, he attempted a melodramatic backwards swoon, almost pulling Maggie down with him. She shook her head, and left alone to his devices, Sam began stomping around irrhythmically. He grasped one of his sister's hands but pulled too hard, and she began to cry, though Sam denied he'd done anything wrong. "What?" he kept saying. "What?"

"Oh, please, Sam," I heard Maggie say, and he went into a sulk.

Mission accomplished. Sam approached me with a pack of playing cards. "Hey, Dad, d'you want to play crazy eights?" he shouted over the music.

"You don't want to dance?" I shouted back.

Sam shook his head rapidly. "I'm *watching*. Crazy eights?" he shouted again.

"Dance!" I mouthed. "You! Go dance!"

"But *you're* not dancing!" Sam shouted back.

"C'mere," I said, and I herded him into the other room. Sam sat down with relief on the couch, but when he started dealing cards, I stopped him. "You know, dancing's *fun*."

"I hate dancing. Dad, how many cards do you deal in crazy eights? Or we could play war or twenty-one instead?"

"You've never danced before in your life, so how do you know if it's fun or not fun?"

"I just know I wouldn't like it, that's all." Sam glanced downward. Then, "I don't know *how* to dance."

"So I'll teach you."

A smile was beginning to form. "But it's so *stupid.*"

"Look, *nobody* knows how to dance. You just go out there, and you do your thing. Nobody's really watching. Nobody really cares."

"So why aren't *you* dancing?"

For the exact same reasons you're not, I wanted to say, *which is why I want you to dance.* Sam's behavior on the dance floor, his shyness, his stiff posture, felt painfully familiar. I didn't want him to be like me as a kid—self-conscious, ironic, sitting life out. But what kind of crummy example was I setting?

"Because just like you, I'm scared of looking like an idiot. Just like you. It's easier to watch, isn't it?" Think about the Beatles (it was hard not to, with "When I Get Home" blaring in the background). Were Paul McCartney or John Lennon *worried* what people thought of them when they stood onstage? Did it really matter in the long run? "Do you know what one of the great things about getting older is?" I shouted.

"What?" Sam shouted back.

"You stop caring as much what other people think about you!"

Sam just stared at me.

"Maybe if we do it together, it wouldn't be so bad. We could kind of cover each other."

Sam shook his head.

"Please?" I said.

"You're a boy," he said at last. "Or a man. Or whatever."

"So what?" I held out my hand. "Here, look: do exactly what I do."

He refused to dance, but he wouldn't let go of my hand.

The kids didn't get to bed until midnight. Sam was toting a new accessory: the four Beatles LPs we'd dragged down from the attic. They sat on the bathroom counter as he brushed his teeth. They accompanied him when he trotted into the kitchen for a glass of water. Finally, they settled in for the night beside his pillow. "You know what makes me really sad?" I said to him. "That you'll never grow up having records. To *hold*, and to *stare at*. CDs just aren't the same."

"What does it mean, 'Rubber Soul'?" Sam asked.

"I think it's another John Lennon pun. Something about the bottom of your shoes."

"I don't understand."

Well, neither did I, actually. Soul, I told him, referred to blues-derived music from the American South, a music that influenced the Beatles as well as other British bands, like the Rolling Stones and Led Zeppelin. (Later, Sam would fill in the rest: in the mid sixties Paul McCartney heard one Southern musician describe the music of his U.K. counterparts as "Plastic Soul." Attracted as ever to any play on words, John altered the two words to "Rubber Soul," then spelled out the title in a shoe shape on the cover of the LP.)

Sam's sisters were sleeping in his room that night, and as

they slid under the covers, Maggie mentioned that I'd forgotten to turn off the bedroom light and that there were now about a hundred gnats on the ceiling.

"Don't be mean to my dad," Sam said. His voice was surprisingly irate.

Maggie was taken aback, as I was. She wasn't being mean, she explained gently.

"Dad forgot," Sam said, "that's all." He shoved the LPs over to make a clearing beside his pillow. "Dad, you can sit here. Leave my dad alone," he ordered, to the girls in the room.

I woke at four-thirty in the morning to find him standing in the dark next to my bed. As my eyes adjusted to the light, I could see his eyes were damp and his mouth was trembling. "Dad," he whispered, "I had a bad dream."

"What'd you dream about?"

Silhouetted against the light from the hall, he shook his head faintly. His dark, extra-large *Titanic* T-shirt made him look goblinlike.

"Do you think you can sleep again, or are you too scared?"

He shook his head: sleep wasn't going to happen. I began dozing off, but then I heard a loud, reproaching sniff.

Except for a few crickets chirping from outside the open windows, the living room was silent. I dragged a quilt in from one of the bedrooms, started a pot of coffee, and when it was done, poured myself a huge cup. We sat on the couch, facing the water, with the quilt draped over our knees. Now that he had company, Sam seemed in a much better mood. "Uggghhh," he said, watching me sip my coffee. "How can you stand drinking that stuff?"

"Because it gets me going in the morning, that's why."

"I'm never going to drink coffee in my life."

"Me, neither. It's disgusting."

"But you're drinking it right now."

I smiled apologetically.

He leaned into my side as the first purple appeared outside and the water began to lighten. The lazing, bony weight of him against me felt nice. I was reminded of how guilty I felt when we had a second baby. Not that Sam didn't want a brother or a sister. And it wasn't that Maggie and I didn't want another kid, either. It was just that by having a second kid we'd put an end to our threesome. It almost felt as though we'd betrayed him.

"Dad," Sam said suddenly, "what's your favorite Beatles song?"

I didn't really know, I told him; there were too many. "The thing about the Beatles is that ninety-eight percent of their songs are good." I paused for a moment. "Actually, you don't even know if they're good because you know them so well. And they're so wrapped around your memories." But I told him a few of my favorites: "Two of Us," and "I Am the Walrus," "Getting Better," and "A Day in the Life." "So what about you?" I asked. "What's *your* favorite Beatles song? I mean, granted, you haven't heard all that many."

Sam didn't hesitate. "The one that goes—" and he hummed it.

I was taken aback by his choice—"In My Life"—but at

the same time, not surprised. It fit who he was: tender, philosophical. "I love that song, too," I said. "You know, John Lennon wrote that."

"John didn't write that. Paul did."

I was amazed that Sam already had such a strong notion of which songs went with which Beatle.

"No, he didn't. John did. The words, at least. I think Paul may have helped out with the middle part of the melody."

Utter incredulity. "John wrote 'In My Life'?"

"See, John's not all *that* bad."

Most people, I told Sam, were complicated. And contradictory (I had to explain *contradictory*). They were a mixture of darkness and innocence, selfishness and charity, sentimentality and cynicism—well, at least the interesting ones were. Many critics and fans considered John Lennon the Beatles' "real" artist, as opposed to Paul. (Why? Sam wanted to know.) Because people had fixed conceptions of what artists should be: rebellious, rule breaking. Which wasn't entirely fair. Paul, after all, had come up with the concepts of *Sgt. Pepper* and *Magical Mystery Tour* and written some of the Beatles' most recognizable songs. "It's true," I said, "that Paul doesn't always dig deeply inside himself. He can be glib. Who can't be? But a musician can't write a killer song every single time. I mean, we sit here judging Paul when most of us can't even write *one* song. Even a bad one."

"I guess not." Sam stretched out his legs under the quilt, then proudly showed me a bruise on his forearm. He'd fallen out of his bed in his sleep, he said, though he'd simply picked himself up and gone back to sleep. "Well, until I woke up again," he added.

I asked him what his bad dream was about.

"I dreamed—" Sam hesitated. "I don't really know."

"Awww, c'mon, tell me."

A long silence. "I dreamed," he said finally, "that you and Mom broke up."

"We did? Why would she and I do something like that?"

He didn't answer. In my own childhood, a few dark expressions scared me witless. An act—*crucifixion*—a leader —*Hitler*—and three common, eavesdropped-on terms: *Cancer. Nervous breakdown. Divorce.* "Mom and I aren't going to break up, Sam," I said finally. "You don't have to worry about that."

"How do you know?"

"Because we're happy. And I love my family. It's just not going to happen."

"The Beatles broke up."

Ah, yes they did.

"It's different," I said. Imagine, I continued, being stuck in a car with the same people, year in and year out. And having to agree on the songs you sang and played. "The Beatles were like brothers," I said to Sam. "They'd known one another since they were thirteen, fourteen years old. They'd gotten rich together. They'd gotten incredibly famous together." I repeated: being a Beatle may have looked like fun, but the reality was different. "Very few people in the history of the world have been as famous as they were. In fact, people who claim to be famous today don't even know what fame *is*. When you're that famous, you can't walk down the street. You can't go to the drugstore and buy toothpaste—"

"Were the Beatles the most famous people ever?"

"Well, just about."

"Were they more famous than God?"

"No, God's a bit more famous."

And then I offered another reason for the Beatles' breakup: the women. Sometimes, I said to Sam, when you fell in love with a woman, your friendships with other men fell by the wayside. "Everything you were ever able to talk about with your best friend, now you can talk about with the woman you're in love with. Plus, you can kiss her too. I mean, you could do that with a boy, but—"

"Yeah, I know, Dad—" Sam interrupted, waving away further explanation.

"Exactly."

The rocky outer islands were starting to take shape.

"There's a movie maybe you'll see someday called *Let It Be*," I went on. "Basically, it shows the Beatles arguing with one another about guitar solos and songs and who plays what, and it ends with a rooftop concert. But one of the big reasons they're all so angry at each other is that John brought Yoko along to the studio with him, and she's quietly watching everything they do. None of the other Beatles wants to say to John, 'Um, John, could you maybe not bring Yoko to rehearsals, because it cramps everybody's style?' But what they're thinking is, '*She's* not a Beatle! *She's* not one of us! And she—this *stranger*—has the nerve to sit there and give us criticism and feedback about our music? *I don't think so.'*"

Sam pondered this for a moment. "So it was the wives' fault."

"No. It was a natural change in the Beatles' lives. In *all* men's lives. Don't forget, Sam, these guys were only twenty-eight, twenty-nine years old. It was time to take the next step, which is usually getting married and having kids. It'll happen to you, too, someday. You'll grow up. You'll make great friends. You'll think, this won't ever change. And then you know what happens? It *changes.*"

It would have been any woman, I explained to Sam, but because it was the Beatles, and everything they did was public, Yoko and Linda got the blame.

Here comes the sun. Literally, there it was, poking up over the outer beach. Downstairs, the furnace shifted; birds sounded; the day was cracking through.

Was I talking too much? Going over Sam's head? But he seemed to be taking in everything I said. "When you fall in love with someone, your friends can feel angry and left out. Guys feel frustrated that they can't give to their friends what a woman does. And you can't really talk about it with your friend, either."

"Why can't you?"

"Because a person will always be most loyal to the man or woman they're in love with." My male friends and I never really talked about our wives. Unless something was going terribly wrong, our wives were generally off-limits. "Which is why when the Beatles broke up they had to criticize one another in code. George wrote a song called 'Not Guilty.' On his solo album *Ram,* Paul wrote a song called 'Too Many People,' which John took as a disguised attack on him and Yoko. To get back at him, John wrote a song called 'How Do You Sleep?' on his *Imagine* album. I think it was because they all felt — well — helpless. Because it wasn't just that the Beatles were over, it was that their *friendship* was over."

"*Can we really live / without each other?*" was a lyric written thirty years after the breakup, when the three remaining Beatles united to complete a partially finished John Lennon song, *Free As a Bird.* "That line gets me every time," I said. "I don't know anybody who's a member of a family — either as a kid, or as a parent — who hasn't wondered that, Sam," I concluded.

Had he and I ever had a conversation this long? I was reminded that unlike my father's and mine, my generation and Sam's intersected on countless cultural fronts. This wasn't the musically moral gulf that existed between Benny Goodman and the Talking Heads, Bix Beiderbecke and Smokey Robinson, Glenn Miller and Patti Smith. No, Sam and I had music in common — lots of it. Movies. Books. Slang. Attitudes. Temptations. There wasn't a whole lot he could confront that I hadn't crashed into myself in my teens and twenties.

Sam stretched his bare heels into the fabric of the couch. "I'm not going to leave, Dad," he said presently.

"Leave where?"

"Just leave. I'm not going to."

I stared at him. "You may change your mind someday. And if you do, that's OK, too."

"I'm not going to leave," Sam repeated.

It was morning. The sun bunched and wrinkled in the branches. Dew on the lawn gleamed. High tide submerged the marsh, except for a few tips.

Sam rose, went into the kitchen, and came back holding a bowl of blackberries. He held them out. "You want one?" he asked.

I took a couple and thanked him. And then I noticed he was staring at me. Finally he balled one hand into a fist, then brought it in slow motion toward my shoulder until it brushed my skin. "Po-o-o-w-w-w-w," he said portentously. Then, raising one arm into the air, his mouth a flat line, he brought his hand down sword-like in slow motion onto the top of my knee. His eyes were ardent, shining, locked on me. He came at me again. I understood suddenly: all his body weaponry—the armbone-sword, the bladed hand, the mock warring expression; all these were dusky substitutions for contact. He wanted me. That's all. Women sometimes found guys hard to figure out, I thought, as I tucked an arm around my son and pulled him toward me, but ultimately, you simply had to learn our code.

3.
Magical
Mystery
Tour

L ESS THAN SEVENTY-TWO HOURS after he'd first heard *Abbey Road*, Sam was hooked. It was as though he'd tumbled through a hole into a mysterious country removed from his life, but recognizable, too. He'd always gotten along better with adults than with other kids, always been fascinated with music and popular culture, and now he'd found his element: famous grownups playing great music. Yes, I'd expected Sam to like the Beatles—who doesn't like them?—but I hadn't anticipated a slam dunk, and neither had Maggie.

On the drive home from the country, we must have listened to *Abbey Road* half a dozen times, followed by two old Beatles cassettes I'd dug up in the basement—*Help!* and *Please Please Me*. Nobody else minded. Sam had brought my old Beatles LPs along with him and, ignoring his Gameboy, spent most of the ride poring over their covers and calling out questions. "Is Shirley Temple still alive?" and "If a person is left-handed, is it hard for them to shake hands?" and "Is there really a place called 'Abbey Road'?"

After we got resettled in our house, Sam rushed to the piano. He'd been taking lessons for the past year, though usually it took a forklift and cable plow to get him to practice. Not tonight. And it wasn't Bartók or "Red River Valley" that came out of the piano but instead, a bobbling, patchwork medley of "Maxwell's Silver Hammer" and "You Never Give Me Your Money."

I sat next to him on the bench. "That's amazing," I said. "How did you figure out how to play those songs?"

"It was just inside my head," Sam said, shrugging. Then, "So, Dad . . . how does 'You Never Give Me Your Money' go again?"

I sang a few halting bars but stopped when Sam began picking out the notes. Two minutes later, he nailed it. He sat back, pleased with himself. "You don't know any other Beatles songs I could play, do you?"

We'd never sat down together before like this on the piano bench. Music lessons were Maggie's department. I'd quit the instrument when I was twelve, impatient with scales and proper fingering.

For the first time in years, I lowered my fingers onto the keys and clumsily sounded out the first few bars of "Maxwell's Silver Hammer."

"You play the bottom, Dad," Sam broke in happily, "and I'll play the top."

We were fumbling and off-key at first, but eventually our styles—his precise, mine monotonously rhythmic—came into sync, and we were playing "Maxwell's Silver Hammer." Sam was a good teacher, infinitely forgiving. "Sorry," I would say whenever I flubbed a note, and he'd lecture me: "Dad, please stop saying 'sorry.' You just do your best job, that's all. If you mess up, you play through it." At one point, he placed his fingers over my larger ones, and showed them where to go.

We played for about an hour, until dinner.

I think back on that duet a lot. Me pounding out the deep-voiced bottom, Sam savoring the childlike top. As we played, I recalled something I knew intuitively: guys usually can't go it alone, one-on-one. We need a topic, a medium, a way in, a third party in the room to spark conversation. Video games, chess, baseball, movies, a hike up a mountain, women of course. But I'd hardly expected a rock group to take on that role.

Even when I left the piano, Sam kept playing. He couldn't quite master the middle notes of "Maxwell's Silver Hammer," but he kept at it. "I have to *learn* this," he told me. It was a point of vanity and also of proprietorship. Just as Sam was proud to claim Ringo as his contemporary (thanks to *Thomas the Tank Engine*), so he now wanted to take possession of the Beatles through the piano—to internalize them. From that day on, Sam lost his reluctance to practice.

The next day, I picked Sam up from school, and we ambled back home. Was I imagining it or did he seem brighter, sharper, less blurry? He had, he told me, the best news. It

seemed his *teacher* had heard of the Beatles. So had most of
the kids in his class. Show and Tell was three days away.
Would it be OK if he brought in *Abbey Road*?

Absolutely, I said. He could find it somewhere in the CD
case downstairs. Sam hesitated. *Abbey Road,* the original LP,
is what he meant. "Most of these kids have probably never
seen a real record album before," he said hanging his head.
"It's kind of sad."

These kids—I loved that.

"Dad, could you show me everything that you and Mom
have of the Beatles?" Sam asked me that afternoon.

He stood next to me as I picked out what we owned—
*Sgt. Pepper's Lonely Hearts Club Band, Magical Mystery Tour,
Please Please Me, Abbey Road, Meet the Beatles, Beatles for
Sale, The White Album,* and *Let It Be.* "Here," I said, hand-
ing him the stack. "You can have them to keep, actually."

"You're *giving* them to me?"

"Well, sure. Everything I own is yours, too. Except you
have to let me listen to them occasionally."

Sam still couldn't swallow it. "Are you positive?" I nodded. "Dad, you can listen to them *anytime* you want. You
don't even have to *ask* me." Sam hesitated. "So is this, like,
all they ever did?"

Well, pretty much. One thing, though: I explained that
each individual Beatle had recorded a bunch of solo albums
after the band's breakup, and that often these albums contained songs written during the band's heyday that the
other three had voted down as being inappropriate for the
Beatles—Paul McCartney's "Junk," John Lennon's "Cold

Turkey," and George Harrison's "All Things Must Pass" being three such examples. "If you wanted to stretch the point a little, you could kind of consider those solo LPs to be Beatles albums, too. In fact, one of these days . . ." but fearing I might be going over his head, I didn't finish.

"One of these days what?"

I explained that I'd always wanted to make a tape of all my favorite solo-Beatles songs. "It would be like the Beatles album they never made together."

Sam took this in soberly.

For a long time, he stood at the base of the stairs, rocking slightly on the soles of his sneakers, the stack of CDs gripped in both hands. His hair came down into his eyes, and he blew it upward with a single puff, as if expelling a feather. *Beautiful boy,* I couldn't help thinking, with a nod to John Lennon. I was starting upstairs when Sam's voice stopped me. "Dad, are you busy right now?"

I hesitated. I *was,* actually. "Not really."

"If you want to, you could listen with me."

"I would love that," I said, turning around.

Of the half dozen or so Beatles CDs I'd given Sam, he wanted to hear *Sgt. Pepper* first. Its hectic cover drew his attention, and Maggie had mentioned it to him several times as the Beatles album he absolutely *had* to hear — "It's the most famous one," she'd told him, "and also the one where it all kind of came together." I put it on, and pulled up a chair next to him.

Two of Us

Sam could get fidgety when he listened to music, but not this time. He lay on the couch, listening to *Sgt. Pepper* in a kind of sacramental silence. His sneaker-tops were crossed. His hands rested in a heap atop his navel. Occasionally he would pick up the cover and stare at it, or else follow the antlike funnels of lyrics preprinted on the inside of the CD pamphlet ("The Beatles' putting the lyrics on the album of *Sgt. Pepper* was the first time anybody did that in pop music history," he informed me later).

I had a much harder time keeping quiet. "A Little Help from My Friends." "Lucy in the Sky with Diamonds." "Getting Better." "When I'm Sixty-Four." "Lovely Rita." "Good Morning." "Within You Without You." "A Day in the Life": I could hardly believe Sam was hearing these songs for the first time. I found myself chattering nervously as each song cued up, just as I'd done when I played the Beatles for my father, except this time the roles were reversed. I couldn't stop stealing glances at him or tossing in asides, and now Sam glanced up. "Dad, I don't mean to be rude here, but would you mind not talking?"

"I can't help it!" I said. And I couldn't. I felt the same exultant pride I had over the weekend, as though I'd conjured the Beatles for my son's pleasure. "Do you know what a thrill it is for me to introduce you to these songs?"

Sgt. Pepper ends with a bizarre twenty-second snippet of gibberish that sounds as though Paul is chanting, "Never to be any other way." This intrigued Sam; he insisted on replaying it a dozen times. "What should we play next?" I asked when he'd finally heard enough of this snippet. "*Magical Mystery Tour*? *Revolver*?"

Sam didn't even have to think about it. "*Sgt. Pepper.*"

"You mean, the whole thing all over again? Any particular song?"

He shook his head. "The whole thing again. From the beginning."

The second time around, Sam was more vocal. "Is this John singing?" he asked during "Lucy in the Sky with Diamonds," and when I told him it was, he said, "I can tell because John's voice has this . . . this *sharp thing* about it. But he also sounds tired. Paul sounds a lot more like he has a cold. Except Paul can change his voice around, and John can't. Remember the fourth song, 'Oh! Darling'?" he went on. "When Paul's yelling?" I realized Sam had memorized *Abbey Road*'s song list. "But then he also sings kind of jazzy in 'When I'm Sixty-Four.'"

"And what do you think Ringo sounds like?"

Sam considered this. "He just sounds like a really good guy. And George sounds a little bit like John and a little bit like Paul." A beat. "Dad, what's your favorite song on *Sgt. Pepper*?"

"The second 'Sgt. Pepper' thingie," I said immediately. "I think it's called the 'reprise.'"

Sam beamed. "That's my favorite one, too!"

"Oh yeah, why?"

"I just like it when Paul counts off, 'One, two, three, *fow-ahhh* . . .' at the beginning."

I confessed to Sam that when I was his age, I used to, well, sort of pretend to be Paul in my bedroom mirror, singing just that song. "I would take this hairbrush and use it as my microphone. And I would count off 'one, two, three, *fow-ahhh,*' which I thought was the coolest thing in the world to do." I added, "Part of me still thinks it's the coolest thing in the world to do."

I'd admitted something; it was his turn now. "Dad . . ." Sam started off.

"Uh-huh?"

"The other day when I was playing the piano, I kept thinking to myself I was Paul. And that someday I could maybe be as good as he is."

"If you keep practicing, I'll bet you can be."

"Um, Dad, let's be realistic."

The next afternoon brought more *Sgt. Pepper.* "This is an Indian instrument called the sitar," I said as the sluggish, buzzing "Within You Without You" cued up again. I explained that along with the ukulele, the sitar was George Harrison's lifelong passion. His love of the instrument led him and the other Beatles to travel to India to explore Hindu religions with a man known as the Maharishi Mahesh Yogi.

"The what-a-what?"

"Maharishi Mahesh Yogi. He was a guru."

"What's a guru?"

"Sort of a guy who knows it all. A teacher." In the mid 1960s, I went on, George found himself at a spiritual dead end. He had everything he'd worked so hard to get—fame, money, women, cars, houses—but he was miserable. "Think about it," I said. "What happens when you get everything you've always wanted? What's next?"

I reminded Sam of the time he'd desperately wanted a cast-iron model of the *Titanic*. I bought it for him, but to my surprise, found him ignoring the thing. When I commented on it a few days later, tears came to his eyes. The little *Titanic* had looked beautiful in the store, he sobbed, surrounded by a fleet of other *Titanic*s, but when he brought it home, it just looked . . . ordinary. "I *did* want it," he said. "I promise. It just didn't feel like the *Titanic* when it was in my room."

"It was kind of the same with George," I said now. "He found out that *things* can't make a person happy."

So George sought answers in Eastern religion, in something called transcendental meditation and later in a religion known as Hare Krishna. "The Beatles thought the maharishi had all the answers," I said. "That he could help them live their lives. But in the end, they found out he was just another guy."

I hadn't intended to make a simplistic moral lesson out of this. Really. But one presented itself automatically, as it would again and again with the Beatles. "It's just like parents," I said to Sam. "We seem to have most of the answers—"

Sam laughed, slightly awkwardly. "Parents don't seem to have most of the answers."

"Well, exactly, we don't. Sometimes we do, but not that often."

My father died three years before Sam was born, but for the first time, I began talking about him. About his occasional delight in the Beatles. About how late at night he used to play his clarinet to Benny Goodman and Paul

Whiteman tunes. About his shyness and formality, his style and intellect.

"Did you love your dad?" Sam asked me suddenly.

"Yes," I said, surprised by my own reflexive shyness. "Sure I did. And I guess I always dreamed I'd have a much closer relationship with my own son than my dad had with me."

Sam was silent. "You *do* have a close relationship with me," he said.

"Do I?" I said.

"Dad, we *do*."

"Well, that makes me feel great," I said.

Sam fell silent. "Dad?" he said at last.

I looked up. "Uh-huh?"

"What's a relationship?"

How does any lasting preoccupation come into being? Now that Sam had discovered I could at least masquerade as a pianist, he requested that I keep him company during his nightly practices. "No offense, Mom," he told Maggie. When they were over, he and I would sit down for a low-key Beatles duet: "Yesterday" or "Polythene Pam" or "We Can Work It Out."

Away from the piano, his interest in the Beatles was exploding.

At first it expressed itself as an unquenchable hunger for information. Did Ringo write any songs? Did Sean Lennon ever hang out with the other Beatles' kids? What was the

U.S.S.R.? What was a Savoy truffle? What was a blue jay way? Other questions were more speculative: Did the Beatles pass one another in the street before they were Beatles? Had John (for example) ever eaten at a Liverpool restaurant without knowing that George was eating two tables away? What did I mean by the word *talent*?

"Talent is like a special ability someone is born with," I explained. "Like you're really good at music. Or else you're a really great painter, or you're great with numbers. You could say, for example, that Paul McCartney and John Lennon were extremely talented. That they were born with great musical abilities, and then they practiced and knocked themselves out working, and the rest is history."

Sam hesitated. "Do you think I'm talented?"

Of course he was, I said. "You're good at most things, actually. Like I said, you're a very good piano player. You're smart. You're a great reader. A great speller. You make friends easily—"

Sam interrupted me. "I don't want to be famous, though."

"Why?" I asked.

"That's what George said to his son, Dhani. He said, 'Never be famous.'"

And where had he found this out? Books. There's a library's-worth of Beatles books designed, it seems, for trivia-loving, record-keeping, comparison-obsessed children, particularly male ones. Among the presents Maggie and I bought Sam for his eighth birthday were several slender paperback compilations of factoids about the group. They posed multiple-choice questions, such as: Who was Eleanor Rigby? Who was the Walrus? In the film *Help!*, how did Ringo come into possession of the ring? Another book documented the origins of every song the Beatles ever recorded, and broke down each Beatle's musical contributions into precise percentages, a division Sam happily seized upon. Over the next several months, when I came into his room to say good night, Sam would be poring over them, and often he would fall asleep with one in his hands.

Maggie and I also bought him every single Beatles CD he didn't own already, including the soundtracks to *A Hard Day's Night* and *Help!*, a documentary called *The Compleat Beatles,* and the video of *Yellow Submarine.* We dug up a battered copy of the video of *Let It Be* and watched as the Beatles bickered for an hour and a half, then straggled upstairs for a final concert on the rooftop of Apple's Savile Row studios.

In no time at all, Sam's favorite song had been sidelined in favor of a top-five song list: "In My Life," "Sgt. Pepper's Lonely Hearts Club Band (reprise)," "One after 909," "How Do You Do It?," and "She Came in through the Bathroom Window." It seemed important to him that he and I love the same songs, and for the same reasons, too. When I told him "How Do You Do It?" was a likable enough tune but that I didn't find it exceptional, Sam gave me the same puzzled look I once gave my sister.

One day he announced to me that George Harrison was his favorite Beatle. Forgetting that "Who's Your Favorite Beatle?" is as succinct a psychological test as any ever administered, I assumed at the time that Sam, a fair-minded person, was simply trying to be equitable.

"What about Paul?" I asked.

"Mom likes Paul the most," Sam told me, sounding ruffled. "*Lily* likes Paul. *Susannah* likes Paul," he went on, referring to his sisters; so did his aunt and his homeroom teacher. "Every girl likes Paul the best," he concluded. "Paul, Paul, Paul."

"That doesn't mean you can't like him, too," I said, adding, "I kind of like Paul the best, too."

"I love Paul, but I like George the best."

"Which one of George's songs do you like the best?"

"I don't like George's *music* that much. It's *him* I like."

This was another thing the Beatles had given him: opinions, and a slowly growing fearlessness about expressing them. A few weeks earlier, he and I watched a video of *Amadeus.* Afterward I remarked that Yoko once called Paul McCartney the Salieri to John Lennon's Mozart. Sam shrugged coolly. An expression of critical distaste came over his face—I'd never seen it before. "If anybody is Salieri," he said, "I think it's Yoko Ono."

His newfound attraction to George was guarded, respectful. He left him alone. "George is private," he explained when I asked why he'd chosen to write Paul, and not George, a letter. "I'm not sure he would like getting mail from people. And I know he wouldn't write me back. Plus," he went on, referring to news reports about a possible recurrence of George's cancer, "people who are sick just want to lie in bed and read and watch TV."

A change in his favorite Beatle wasn't the only shift I noticed in him. The most obvious one was taking place in our relationship. "Marriage is a long conversation," Robert Louis Stevenson wrote once, and the Beatles were, too. By now our days had taken on a happy, looping choreography. At any time, in any setting, one or the other of us could spontaneously pick up the thread of our ongoing Beatles conversation. We might launch into a discussion about Ravi Shankar or George Martin or Wings. Or, having heard about Paul and Linda's vegetarianism from Maggie, he would ask whether a meatless diet was good for you or whether it simply made you worn out.

Then there were the almost daily quizzes. "Dad," Sam would challenge me first thing in the morning or before bedtime. "Can you name me all the Beatles songs that mention the sun?"

"Uh, 'Here Comes the Sun,'" I'd respond, then falter.

"'I'll Follow the Sun.' And there's 'Rain.'"

"But 'Rain' is about *rain,* not sun."

"The song only has to *mention* the sun."

There were seventeen Beatles songs with the word "sun" in them, Sam informed me. Ten Beatles songs that mentioned the word "rain." Three Beatles songs with the word "diamonds" in their lyrics. He would name them all.

The Beatles led us so effortlessly to other subjects. Christianity and Hinduism (which we'd gotten into when we talked about George and the maharishi, and when he came across John's famous remark that the Beatles were "more popular than Jesus"). Shakespeare (a result of hearing the last few lines of "I Am the Walrus," which John taped off a BBC radio production of *King Lear*). Other singers (after Sam listened to Ella Fitzgerald's version of "Got to Get You into My Life" with mute incredulity, saying finally, "Dad, no offense, I know she has this *perfect* voice, but I think only the Beatles should sing Beatles songs"). The importance of practice (the Beatles' musical apprenticeship in Hamburg). And hard work (as evidenced in the three *Anthology* albums, which contained alternate versions and outtakes of songs most Beatles fans knew note perfectly). It was through the Beatles that Sam learned about Ed Sullivan, Scotland, Amsterdam, Germany, the Philippines, the Who (Ringo's son, Zak Starkey, was the band's drummer), Elvis Presley, Georgie Fame, Chuck Berry, Jimi Hendrix, Mia Farrow, Gideon Bibles, Lewis Carroll, Martin Luther King, Malcolm X, Robert Kennedy, Dylan Thomas, Edgar Allan Poe, and the countless celebrities jostling for position on the cover of *Sgt. Pepper.*

We spent our meals listening to *Revolver* and *Magical Mystery Tour* and discussing somberly what it must be like to be Paul McCartney's son, James, or praising Yoko's shrewd business sense in buying and selling Holstein cows. A stranger eavesdropping on our nighttime discussions might conclude that we'd reached a point of identification with the Beatles that effectively canceled out our own identities. We were like the Beatles ourselves, chatting about the travails, victories, and small disturbances of being us.

As for me, having the Beatles back in my life was, as always, an emotional, guiltless pleasure. I couldn't even tell you what the songs evoked—they were so entwined around four decades of life, mine and other people's. Only Christmas carols filled me with the same mix of happiness and melancholy. It wasn't that the time the songs evoked was upsetting, merely that it was gone. The emotional statute of limitations had expired for me as far as certain tunes were concerned—if Sam made me listen to "Hey Jude" or "The Long and Winding Road" one more time, I was going to jump off the roof—but nearly all of them still had the power to escort me willingly into the past in only two or three bars.

A few weeks later, all five of us repaired to a restaurant to celebrate my birthday. As I was digging into my cheddar-and-bacon potato skins, Sam tapped me on the shoulder, then leaned over to whisper into my ear: "Dad, I have something for you, but I didn't bring it to the restaurant. It's back at home."

"Geez, Sam, thank you."

"D'you want to know what it is?"

"No, that would kill the surprise."

Back in our living room, Sam huddled up beside me on the couch. "So, Dad," he whispered conspiratorially, "will you please come upstairs with me and get your present? Dad and I will be *right back*," he announced to Maggie and his sisters. "Come on, Dad."

We padded upstairs. "So what's the big secret here?" I asked. "Why couldn't we do it downstairs?"

"I just don't think the girls will understand," Sam called over his shoulder. "Mom might, but . . ."

We'd reached his bedroom. Over the past several months, it had been completely transformed. Gone was the dinosaurs-of-the-world poster and the Michael Jordan clock. The Brio tracks were now stacked and crisscrossed in a tub, and the Hot Wheels racing set lay under his bed in orange strips. I'd had to move his bed to accommodate a new CD player and a growing collection of Beatles music and books. Various friends and relatives, who'd caught wind of Sam's new passion, had begun showering him with Beatles paraphernalia, Beatles clothing—a tie here, a T-shirt there—as well as old Beatles albums. The ceiling—dotted with beaming Beatles faces scissored from books and magazines—was a Fab Four solar system. The coin-sized heads, with an occasional violin-shaped Hofner bass guitar or floating drum set thrown in for novelty's sake, provided a collage of unsettling precocity—Paul McCartney was twenty-seven when *Sgt. Pepper* came out, George Harrison even younger.

As for my present, I had no idea what to expect. A watercolor from second-grade art class? Maybe something made out of clay? Or maybe Maggie had slipped him a little money so he could buy, say, a CD or a book. I took a seat at the end of his bed and waited there.

"Dad, close your eyes please."

I heard sounds then, the rustle of something opening and closing and a nestlike weight on my knee, followed by his low command: "OK, open your eyes now."

So I did. On my knee rested a black, unlabeled cassette

in a plastic shell, a glasses case, and a pen. Sam was beaming. "Happy birthday, Dad!" he exclaimed, and threw his arms around me.

I thanked him at length.

"OK, the glasses case is for your glasses. Because you're always losing them, but you can never find them, because you need your glasses to find your glasses, but you see, you've lost your glasses."

"Sam, thank you!"

"And the pen is, well, because you use a pen when you're working."

"I'm always losing my pens, too," I said.

"I bought it with my allowance," he confessed.

Unlike his free-spending sisters, Sam was a scrimper and a saver. "No," I protested, "you shouldn't buy stuff for me with your own money—"

"It was *fun!* Here's the last thing." Sam took a deep breath. "I made us a new Beatles album!"

At first I didn't understand. "But I thought we already *had* everything by the Beatles," I said slowly.

No. Did I remember a while ago, Sam said, when I told him that each Beatle had released various solo albums after the band broke up, that is, *Ram, Imagine, All Things Must Pass, Double Fantasy,* even *Starr*? And that even if you didn't really consider them to be Beatles albums, well, they actually were? OK, what he, Sam, had done was to assemble twenty or so songs from those albums and record them onto a cassette. Basically, he'd made me my own post-Beatles Beatles album. With a little help from Maggie, of course, in choosing some of the songs and showing him how to work the tape player.

"I wrote out a list of the songs, too. I was going to write out all the words, too, but it would take me too long. Mom said you probably know them all anyway."

My brand-new Beatles album went like this:

1. Too Many People
2. All Things Must Pass
3. Cold Turkey
4. Imagine
5. Teddy Boy
6. Uncle Albert/Admiral Halsey
7. That Would Be Something
8. Beware of Darkness
9. You're Sixteen
10. Beautiful Boy
11. My Sweet Lord
12. Maybe I'm Amazed
13. Mother
14. The Songs We Were Singing
15. Bluebird
16. Junk
17. Starting Over
18. Happy Xmas (War Is Over)
19. London Town
20. Instant Karma

I hugged him for a long time. "Thank you *so* much, Sam. God, what a fantastic present."

My son was getting ready for bed now. He brushed his teeth, changed into his Blue Meanies T-shirt, then got under the covers and pulled them up around his neck. In recent weeks, in lieu of a bedtime story, he'd asked me to quiz him from one of his Beatles books, which for the next fifteen minutes, I happily did. What's the name of the real-life person, a friend of John and of Paul's, who "blew his mind out in a car"? Stout heir Tara Guinness. What's the name of the river-hugging town outside London where George Harrison lived? Henley-on-Thames. From "I Am the Walrus," what, precisely, is *semolina*? And while we were on the subject, what's a *pilchard*? (A custard and a kind of sardine, respectively.) Where was *Let It Be* filmed?

"Something like . . . I think it's Twiggy or something?" Sam guessed.

"Twickenham Studios," I corrected.

We finished up; then I crossed the room to put on some music. Even before bedtime, Sam liked to be serenaded by John, Paul, George, and Ringo.

"Dad," Sam said suddenly, "what's an Apple Scruff?"

"An Apple Scruff is a groupie," I said.

"What's a groupie?"

"A groupie is someone who likes to hang around famous people. It's usually a woman, but it can be a man, too. Whenever the Beatles would record at Apple, there would always be girls hanging outside the gate, waiting for the Beatles to come out. George called them 'Apple Scruffs.' Not in a mean way, in a . . . friendly, respectful way. I think he sort of admired their persistence."

"Were there any boys?"

"Yes. Boys and girls both. But more girls I'd say. A lot of them were in love with the Beatles."

"But I thought the Beatles were married."

"That didn't really matter to these girls. They just wanted to be around a Beatle, that's all. And a lot of them hated the Beatles' wives. They were very jealous of Linda for marrying Paul, and Yoko for marrying John. They used to call them terrible things."

"Oh."

"Cynthia came home one day, I read once, to find Yoko standing serenely in her kitchen. Imagine if Mom came home one day, and there was another woman in the house, and you were like, 'Excuse me, who are you?'"

"Wait—were John and Cynthia still married?"

"Yes."

"What did Julian say?"

"I don't know, Sam. Julian was probably so young I'm not sure he really understood what was going on."

Sam shook his head wordlessly.

"So what shall we put on tonight?" I asked now. *"Beatles Live at the BBC? Anthology 3?"*

Sam took a long time to answer. He seemed—was it possible—embarrassed. "Dad . . ." he said finally, in a small voice, "would it be all right if you put on Raffi?"

I felt a rush of empathy for him. Kneeling down beside his bed, I told him he could listen to whatever he wanted, whether it was the Spice Girls, Pete Seeger, Beethoven, or the Singing Nun. "I think I'd go nuts if I listened to the Beatles all the time," I said.

Sam nodded; these were words he wanted to hear. Relieved, happy now, he hiked his covers up farther. To my surprise, I'd kind of missed Raffi myself, and now I slipped the *Baby Beluga* cassette into the tape recorder and prepared to reenter a long-gone world of peanut butter sandwiches, noisy ducks, and bumblebees.

I had to remind myself: this new Beatles country Sam had stumbled onto this year wasn't always the most hospitable place to visit. It had insanely intricate relationships, sharp divisions, competitions, hurt feelings, rivalry, money, fame, ambition, reinvention, bitchiness, and breakup. Sometimes you had to take a time-out. Go for a walk. Clear your head. And listen to music that had no real context other than your own childhood, your own tight family. He was only eight, after all.

4.
Beatles
for
Sale

" **H** ULLO," said the shaggy-haired man in the light blue satin brocaded jacket. "I'm Sir Paul." He had circles under sleepy, Mediterranean eyes and a meaty handshake. A prop-Hofner bass guitar protruded from under his left arm. "I didn't catch your name . . ."

"Sam," he said shyly. "Sam Smith."

"Sam, are you interested in posing for a photo with me?"

"No, thank you."

Sir Paul's lopsided accent was half Liverpool, half why-bother. With his over-the-ears coiffure and ingratiatingly thumbs-up manner, he did in fact resemble Paul McCartney.

He explained to Sam and me how he'd fallen into this

line of work. "Nobody noticed the resemblance when I was younger," he said. "I was a lot thinner back then. It wasn't until I'd put on forty pounds—I went on the seafood diet: I *see food,* and then I eat it—that people began commenting on how much I looked like the real Paul." He pivoted in place. "Hullo," he said to another passerby, "I'm Sir Paul of Livermore."

Sam was yanking on my sleeve. "Can I please go look around?" and when I nodded, he loped off into the crowd. A few minutes later, I found him seated in front of a Beatles laser karaoke video booth, unable to tear his eyes away from an elderly woman, her rail-thin thirtyish son, and her middle-aged daughter singing and strumming along to a recording of "While My Guitar Gently Weeps." Behind them, a wide-screen video monitor parted and swirled psychedelically.

"Are you having a good time?" I whispered.

"Dad," Sam whispered back with polite disbelief, "these people are *insane.*"

We were among the thousands of paying attendees at the New York–New Jersey Beatlefest. A weekend event, it offered fans a groaning board of Beatle-related merchandise, contests, and activities: a Beatles marketplace, with nearly one hundred tables on display, and vendors from as far away as Japan and Canada; a Beatles museum and art contest; nonstop screenings of Beatles films and videos; a Battle of the Beatles Bands contest; a Beatles sound-alike contest; a Beatles trivia game show; a Beatles photo exhibit; a Beatles memorabilia exhibit; the aforementioned laser karaoke booth; a display of original artwork, one by John Lennon and the other by Klaus Voorman, who'd recently designed the covers of the *Anthology* CDs; a detailed discussion of Beatles fan fiction; and even a Beatles puppet show.

Beatlefest was my idea. I'd found out about this nearly three-decade-old phenomenon on the Internet in the course of researching a trivia question Sam had posed (whether it was true that George Harrison had a sign on his front door that read, "Please Go Away" — the answer was yes), and I thought, *Why not?* If Sam was such a fanatic, why not surround him for seventy-two hours with other Beatles lovers? If nothing else, he might discover he wasn't alone. "Hey, Sam, do you have any interest in going to something called Beatlefest?" I called out. "It's a weekend festival devoted to the group."

"Sure," came his voice from the next room. I impulsively bought tickets online, then appeared in Sam's bedroom doorway to tell him we'd be attending all three days. "So will Paul and George be there?" Sam asked excitedly.

"No."

"Ringo?"

"No," I said, feeling ashamed for having unintentionally misled him. "It's for Beatles' *fans,* actually."

"Oh," he said, "darn." Then he beamed. "Dad, I was just *kidding* you."

On a raw Saturday morning a few weeks later, Sam and I journeyed into Manhattan and then east over to Bloomingdale's department store, where I'd reserved tickets on a shuttle bus that would take us into Secaucus, New Jersey. When eleven o'clock came around, and the bus still hadn't arrived, I approached one of the dozen or so women I saw clustered around the store's Third Avenue entrance. Most had a long-suffering clerical look about them, mixed with eccentric touches — go-go boots, a heart-shaped purse, a lapel pin reading "Jesus Loves You But I'm His Favorite."

"Excuse me," I said, "but is this where people wait for the Beatlefest bus?"

"Oh, hold on a sec here," the woman said. "Is this your first time?" Hesitantly, I nodded. *"Beatles virgins!"* she exploded. "Hey, everybody — we have a couple of *Beatles virgins* right here!"

There was whooping and whistling and clamorous applause. One of the women began pounding the side of her handbag, trying to get a rhythm going. Another came toward me with her hand raised, and I recoiled, only to realize that all she wanted to do was give Sam and me matching high-fives.

Sam looked appropriately baffled. "Dad, what do they mean by 'Beatles virgins'?" he whispered.

Thinking fast, I whispered back, "It's someone whose first time it is at something," and left it at that.

The final passenger count on the Beatlefest bus was: females, fifteen; males (including Sam and me), four. The two other guys said nothing during the ride, and instead, read their paperback mysteries and stared out the window. But the women were raucous and wouldn't stop talking. When the bus bumped over a pothole-heavy patch of a New York City street, three of them began beating their fists against their chests while making Tarzan yells.

As the anthology went on, the stories got longer and stranger. In "I'm Talkin' 'Bout Girls Now," Paul awakens in a hotel room to discover that overnight he's turned into a woman named Paula (with "breasts . . . oh, very nice lovely," as well as fully intact "lower implications"). The other three Beatles have turned into women, too: Georganne, JoAnne, and Rachel. In the final story, a group of Orthodox rabbis is startled to receive a flurry of e-mails along HaKotel HaMaaravi, one of Israel's most revered sites, all pertaining to George Harrison's deteriorating health.

Sam was gazing blankly at the crowds still pushing their way toward the convention hall. "What are you thinking about?" I asked.

"It's just *interesting* . . ." he trickled off.

"No, what, tell me."

"I'm *thinking*." Sam hesitated, then said, "It's just interesting that I'm not the only person who's into the Beatles, that's all."

"Is that a good feeling?" I asked.

Sam looked a little pained. "Sort of."

We finished our lunch and stood up. But where should we go now? *Home* is where I really wanted to be, but checking my watch, I saw that the shuttle bus didn't leave for another nine and a half hours. A three-foot-tall, mustachioed man in a buttery yellow Sgt. Pepper's uniform trotted past us, followed by a nurse serenely pushing a goateed man in a wheelchair. By now, the carnal, collegial aroma of hot dogs, pretzels, and beer suds was gusting in over our heads.

Taking Sam's hand, I ducked into a dark auditorium plastered with neon-lit blowups of the Beatles' record covers, as well as giant, psychedelically blinking cartoon images of Paul, John, George, and Ringo. "The Beatles' use of Roman numerals predates the Super Bowl," the man onstage was saying, "thereby adding yet another feather to the Fab Four's crown of 'firsts.'"

"Can we go someplace else?" Sam whispered, so he and I snuck back out into the lobby again. Riffling through my program, I saw that if we made a dash for it, we could catch the beginning of the Beatles talent show, known as "Beatles Opportunity Knocks!"

I showed Sam the program. "That could be fun," he said with a shrug. "Except I don't really like exclamation marks that much. They're sad."

"I know what you mean," I said softly.

This hall was standing room only. Sam and I found our way to the back of the room, then slid down the wall onto the floor. "Is this OK?" I asked him. "I mean, at least we get a little cross-breeze down here." But as more and more people filed in, we found ourselves unable to see farther than two feet ahead of us.

A potbellied emcee stepped onstage, his voice heavily miked. The first contestant, he announced, would be performing an acoustic guitar version of "I Am the Walrus." "Beatles Opportunity *Knocks!*" the emcee bawled.

There was tumultuous applause mixed in with a few beery whoops. The contestant, a thin, timid-looking man, took the stage to perform a lilting guitar version of John Lennon's phantasmagoric song. The audience's applause was tepid. The next performer, also shy-looking and male, sang a wobbling "Mother Nature's Son."

Sam tapped me on the shoulder. "Hey, Dad," he whispered, "do you want to play hangman?"

"Sure," I whispered back. "You think up something, and I'll try to guess it."

Diligently, Sam drew the lines on which to write the letters for seven words, followed by a question mark. Then he sketched in a small platform, a brace, and a squiggle meant to symbolize the noose. "OK, Dad," he hissed, "guess away."

"A."

Sam drew in three *A*s.

"E."

There were three *E*s.

Beginner's luck. I missed with the next guesses. The hangman now had two eyes, a mouth, and an arm. But after a couple more guesses, the word, or the saying, or whatever it was, was also taking shape. I studied it:

I/_A_E/_ _ _ _/_A_/_E/P_ E A _ E/G_?

"I don't know what that says," I whispered.

"You will."

"Oh, wait, I forgot to ask," I said. "Is this a person or a place or a thing?"

"It's none of those things," Sam said darkly.

I called out a few more letters. *H* was the first letter of the second word. *G* began the last one. And then, in a flash, I saw exactly what he'd spelled out. It wasn't a proper name, a place, a country, a continent, a saying, or an aphorism. It was a plea from a tortured heart:

"I HATE THIS. CAN WE PLEASE GO?"

• • •

"Dad," Sam said solemnly as we were boarding the Manhattan-bound commuter bus that left every half-hour from a nearby bus stop, "thank you very, very much. For taking me, and for the ticket, and all that."

"Oh, you're very welcome."

"But, Dad . . ." Sam paused. "You must never, ever take me to something like that again."

"Let It Be" was playing in the midtown Manhattan coffee shop where Sam and I ended up. Over the past few months, he'd been happy to find, if he'd ever doubted it, that the Beatles were as famous, and as ubiquitous, as Maggie and I always claimed they were. "Here's one," he'd call out from the living room whenever he heard "When I'm Sixty-Four" on a TV commercial, or "Get Back" in a radio ad, or "Love Me Do" serenading the local Starbucks.

"They're everywhere," I said to Sam now as we sat drinking ginger ales and listening to "Let It Be." "There's just no escaping the Beatles." At my prompting, he ordered a steak as his reward for surviving Beatlefest.

The steak arrived, and Sam dove into it. "I didn't know there were so many people who were so crazy about the Beatles," he said between bites.

"Well, I certainly was. Mom was. We still are. And let's not forget you. Maybe not to the extent you saw today . . ."

"I love the Beatles and all, but . . ." Sam tried to put it into words. "I love other things, too."

"Sam, you have to understand that when I was eight years old, the Beatles were the coolest people in the world. They introduced me to England, to long hair, to girls. They

Sam sat in the seat across from me, quietly playing Super Mario on his Color Gameboy. I leaned over to the woman in the adjoining seat. "So is this *your* first Beatlefest, too?"

Janie—as she introduced herself—was wearing flamboyant pink lipstick and a roomy black sweatshirt with the legend *Beatles Forever* across its front. No, she'd been going to Beatlefests for twenty years now. "They're a blast," she sighed. "I envy you that it's your first time."

"They're Beatles virgins," the woman next to her broke in, and several others nodded in cheerful confirmation.

Sam maxed out on his thirty-minute Gameboy limit. For the rest of the trip, through New Jersey's sprawling Meadowlands—reedy former swampland where teals, pintails, and Canadian geese share living space with abandoned industrial parks and rusted train tracks—he and I played hangman.

Sam's answers were all Beatles connected. One was "I Am the Walrus." Another was "The Fool on the Hill." A third was "Stella McCartney Makes Clothes." In the middle of our fifth straight game, the bus pulled to a squeaking stop in front of the Meadowlands Crowne Plaza Hotel. It was approximately noon. We scrambled out, ladies first.

The return trip into Manhattan, the driver told me, left promptly at 11 P.M.

"Oh," I said, my heart sinking.

The line of people waiting to get into Beatlefest stretched halfway out the door of the Crowne Plaza Hotel. Sam and I took up position by the far wall, fearful of getting trampled underfoot. I leafed through the thick Beatlefest catalogue. "Anything you want to do in particular?" I asked.

"Could we maybe get something to eat?"

"Sure," I said, "but wait one sec; what about you and I aim to catch the 2 P.M. lecture on 'The Beatles in Rishikesh'?"

Sam squinted as he tried to recall what Rishikesh was. When I reminded him it was the Indian village where the Beatles met up with the maharishi, he shook his head softly. "No offense, Dad, but that sounds boring."

"How about a lecture called 'Inside the Yellow Submarine'? Or here's one: 'I Went to LIPA.'"

"What's a 'LIPA'?"

"The Liverpool Institute of Performing Arts. Wait, that sounds a little—I don't know—obscure." In the end, I suggested that maybe he and I could wander around until we found our bearings.

We slowly pushed our way into the exhibit hall and began wading through the aisles. The approximate size of a soccer field, the room was jammed with people, pushing forward, elbowing one another aside, or crunched up against the display tables as if waiting to snatch bags from a luggage carousel. The vendors stood patiently behind their tables. Most had the slack, world-weary look of lifelong carnies. Almost everybody I bumped into or squeezed past or stepped on by accident was wearing a piece of clothing with some form of Beatles insignia on it—an *Abbey Road* T-shirt stretched over a keg-stomach, a *Revolver* necktie, a belt with green apples dancing across it. God only knew about their underwear and socks.

At one point, Sam turned around. "Dad, *don't* lose me, please. I'd never find my way out of here again."

Together, we bullied our way through the clothing section, past Beatles caps, tank tops, T-shirts, gym shorts, boxer shorts, neckties, visors, sweatpants, hooded sweatshirts, and "high-density muscle-tees" in all colors and styles and graphics, ranging from the basic ("Let It Be") to the nauseating (the Beatles standing in what looked like Heaven). There were sweatshirts reading "I Feel Fine" and "Yeah! Yeah! Yeah!" and the faintly needy "Help!" There were Beatles thermoses, lunchboxes, watches, cups, travel mugs, picture frames, banks, plates, boxes, lamps, calendars, socks, blankets, money clips, magnets, belt buckles, backpacks, wristwatches, mouse pads, musical globes, tea sets, bookends, beanie bears, model kits, inflatable chairs, puzzles, candles, trading cards, stamps, headbands, key chains, mini gumball sets, and Christmas ornaments, as well as a comprehensive line of "John Lennon Art–inspired stationery, photo books, and gift items," which included postcards and ceremonial coins. There were Beatles baseballs, Beatles lava lamps, and for about nine thousand dollars, a limited-edition Beatles Yellow Submarine Jukebox.

I'd told Sam he could buy anything he wanted (except for the jukebox), but so far, he'd resisted. Now he turned to me. "Can we go back out into the hallway?" he mouthed.

"Totally!" I mouthed back.

A trio of friendly-looking, bespectacled women flagged us down as we rounded the corner back into the lobby. They were seated behind a table, partially obscured by several stacks of paperbacks. The middle one fixed her attention on me. "Hello," she said brightly. "Are you at all interested in Beatles fan fiction? We have both volumes of our anthology for sale."

Noticing my confusion, she launched into a detailed explanation. Beatles fan fiction brought together in anthology form dozens of short stories about the Fab Four. The editorial board imposed only a few guidelines. Writers should show the proper respect to the Beatles, and remain faithful to their voices, for example, not forget they're English. The board rejected pornography, excessive profanity, as well as any stories "in which any of the Beatles are physically harmed in an excessive and gory manner." And no stalker stories, given what happened to John Lennon. To my surprise, the editorial board discourages any fiction that treats him as a saint.

I cheerfully paid twelve dollars for *Beatles Fan-Fiction, Volume 2,* thanked her, and moved on.

As Sam wolfed down a hot dog from a nearby lunch cart, I leafed through the anthology. In "Cry Baby Cry," the protagonist, admitting that her heart is cold and that "what he needed I couldn't supply," leaves a farewell note on Paul McCartney's pillow, double-checks to see that Martha the sheepdog's water bowl is filled — "You'll be the woman of the house when I leave," she murmurs into the dog's ear — then makes her way to the airport, only to be met there by a distraught but ultimately sympathetic Paul. In "Don't! Pass Me By!" [*sic*] a teenaged Ringo Starr, recovering from a childhood ailment in a hospital, perceives a mysterious, eerily smiling night nurse, who, the reader learns later, is actually Death.

As the anthology went on, the stories got longer and stranger. In "I'm Talkin' 'Bout Girls Now," Paul awakens in a hotel room to discover that overnight he's turned into a woman named Paula (with "breasts . . . oh, very nice lovely," as well as fully intact "lower implications"). The other three Beatles have turned into women, too: Georganne, JoAnne, and Rachel. In the final story, a group of Orthodox rabbis is startled to receive a flurry of e-mails along HaKotel HaMaaravi, one of Israel's most revered sites, all pertaining to George Harrison's deteriorating health.

Sam was gazing blankly at the crowds still pushing their way toward the convention hall. "What are you thinking about?" I asked.

"It's just *interesting* . . ." he trickled off.

"No, what, tell me."

"I'm *thinking*." Sam hesitated, then said, "It's just interesting that I'm not the only person who's into the Beatles, that's all."

"Is that a good feeling?" I asked.

Sam looked a little pained. "Sort of."

We finished our lunch and stood up. But where should we go now? *Home* is where I really wanted to be, but checking my watch, I saw that the shuttle bus didn't leave for another nine and a half hours. A three-foot-tall, mustachioed man in a buttery yellow Sgt. Pepper's uniform trotted past us, followed by a nurse serenely pushing a goateed man in a wheelchair. By now, the carnal, collegial aroma of hot dogs, pretzels, and beer suds was gusting in over our heads.

Taking Sam's hand, I ducked into a dark auditorium plastered with neon-lit blowups of the Beatles' record covers, as well as giant, psychedelically blinking cartoon images of Paul, John, George, and Ringo. "The Beatles' use of Roman numerals predates the Super Bowl," the man onstage was saying, "thereby adding yet another feather to the Fab Four's crown of 'firsts.'"

"Can we go someplace else?" Sam whispered, so he and I snuck back out into the lobby again. Riffling through my program, I saw that if we made a dash for it, we could catch the beginning of the Beatles talent show, known as "Beatles Opportunity Knocks!"

I showed Sam the program. "That could be fun," he said with a shrug. "Except I don't really like exclamation marks that much. They're sad."

"I know what you mean," I said softly.

This hall was standing room only. Sam and I found our way to the back of the room, then slid down the wall onto the floor. "Is this OK?" I asked him. "I mean, at least we get a little cross-breeze down here." But as more and more people filed in, we found ourselves unable to see farther than two feet ahead of us.

A potbellied emcee stepped onstage, his voice heavily miked. The first contestant, he announced, would be performing an acoustic guitar version of "I Am the Walrus." "Beatles Opportunity *Knocks!*" the emcee bawled.

There was tumultuous applause mixed in with a few beery whoops. The contestant, a thin, timid-looking man, took the stage to perform a lilting guitar version of John Lennon's phantasmagoric song. The audience's applause was tepid. The next performer, also shy-looking and male, sang a wobbling "Mother Nature's Son."

every day. It's as though the Beatles are still a working band who merely happen to be on hiatus. Many of the other Web sites have a clammy, subterranean aura about them, and some afford you glimpses inside private lives that make Eleanor Rigby's seem rich by comparison.

Hey, it's me, Jimbo! Across the universe, I'm still the world's #1 Beatles fan!

Or, *Welcome to Gloria's Fab-tastic world! It's been a hard day's night—so won't you stay awhile?*

I'm sorry, I cannot.

About one thousand Beatles bootlegs were in global circulation, issued by record labels like Swingin' Pig, Wizardo, and Yellow Dog, and bearing names like "The Black Album," "The Lost Pepperland Reel," "Live in Washington," and "Five Nights in a Judo Arena." Here was the strange thing, though: none of these sites mentioned how anybody could actually obtain these bootlegs. The language was masterfully imprecise, except in those cases when it was menacingly specific: *You cannot—repeat, cannot—buy bootlegs here!* more than one site hollered into the void.

Nearly two hours and two dozen dead links later, I came across a Web site that at least offered the possibility of trades. It didn't have to be Beatles music, I was told. It could be the Who, David Bowie, the Rolling Stones, or Led Zeppelin— anything unreleased, privately obtained, or recorded clandestinely under a hat or a raincoat. You sent the guy your bootleg Who or Stones concert, and in return he'd send you "Beatles Ultra Rare Trax" or "The Beatles Live in Paris."

Unfortunately, I had no bootlegs to trade.

Yet, there were provisions for people like me. I could check off my various Beatles selections, then send the proprietor two blank ninety-minute cassettes, and Billy would record what I wanted on one of the cassettes and keep the other for herself. That seemed fair, if a lot of work for Billy. A link opened up three single-spaced pages worth of Beatles bootlegs available for copying. I'd picked five that sounded promising—among them, "The Entire Rooftop Concert," "Live at Candlestick Park," and "Let It Be Rehearsal Tapes #5"—though unfortunately, the Web site hadn't bothered to provide a song list.

"So," I said. "Billy Shears isn't your real name." Any Beatles fan worth his or her salt knew it belonged to the fictitious leader of Sgt. Pepper's Lonely Hearts Club Band.

The girl laughed. "Duhhhh." Then she said suddenly, "Just so you know, this is all illegal. You know that, right?"

"What's illegal?" Was this call being taped?

"Wait. D'you want to know the exact . . . how? Here. I feel like I have to tell everybody. OK—I can say this in my sleep—under U.S. federal law, it is prohibited to buy, sell, manufacture, play, broadcast, or transmit counterfeit recordings. Quote unquote."

"Well, that's that," I said, prepared to throw in the towel. I can be disgustingly licit sometimes. "OK, then—"

"And trading too. Trading's illegal too." Billy Shears went on to explain that most "judges" believed that possession of bootlegs was next to impossible to enforce, not to mention a waste of judicial time, since if you caught a consumer redhanded, he could attempt to prove in court that he had no intention of ever actually listening to the bootleg. *That bootleg over there on the windowsill? It keeps my papers from flying away.* She paused. "Anyhow, I've never known anyone who's gotten into trouble with boots. Cops have a lot better things to do these days, right? You just don't want to be stupid about it. You just don't want to go around advertising the fact on your forehead." A beat, then, "So you wrote you don't have any boots to trade me, right?"

She sounded so disappointed that I heard myself apologizing.

"You can buy stuff off me, too, you know," the girl said, "if you're not into cassettes. I have a CD burner. Wait—" She cupped the receiver and I heard her hollering someone's name, followed by a second fumbled "Wait." Then she was gone for several minutes, before returning breathlessly. "Sorry," she said. "My brother ran off with my price list."

Her rates seemed competitive enough, ranging from fifteen to thirty dollars per CD. In between reeling off the prices, she filled me in a little about the bootleg industry. "Anything that says 'Made in Italy' is shit. Not because Italy's a bad place—it's not, not that I've ever been there, it's supposed to be beautiful—it's just that the sound quality usually isn't very good"; and "You want boots that've been burned off of a master tape. Not some ninth-generation garbage." Something occurred to her. "Hey, this isn't for a Christmas present or anything, is it?"

Christmas was a few days away. "Yeah," I said. "It's for my little boy, actually. He's seven."

"You're kidding me, right?"

"Nope."

A sharp intake of girl breath. "And he loves the Beatles? Oh my God. That's so cool. Will you tell him I said so?" But there was one small problem, it turned out: she wouldn't be able to get the bootlegs to me before December 25. "See, usually people send me a check, and I send them the stuff priority. But first I wait until the check clears, which usually takes three or four days—"

"The check's going to clear," I broke in.

"I'm not saying it won't. I've just had some not-good experiences, that's all."

"Do you take credit cards?"

"No. I'm working on all that, though." Billy hesitated. "Shit, I wish you'd called me up last week or something."

"Awww, he'll be so disappointed," I said.

"He's really seven years old?" she asked.

"Yeah," I said, "and he *adores* the Beatles." I was trying to think of ways to make Sam sound more Dickensian-pitiful than he was. But something had shifted, because now Billy was telling me that she worked "in the city," and she could always deliver them to me in person.

"Well, like, where," I asked, "could we meet?"

"D'you know where Penn Station is?"

"Sure."

This sounded safe (and public) enough. If I was planning on doing something illegal, what could be a better crime scene than a crowded train terminal? Plus, if Billy turned out to be a fed, I could make a cinematic run for it, losing myself in a swarm of commuters. It seemed a minor price to pay to feed my son's Beatles appetite, which, like most addictions, was growing and hungry for more, more, more.

"Oh," she added before hanging up, "I'm kind of small, people tell me I'm cute and that I talk too much."

Billy Shears and I had made a simple plan. At ten minutes to six, I planted myself outside the Penn Station waiting area, which, according to a humorless sign, only valid ticket-holding passengers were permitted to enter. The station resembled the floor of the New York Stock Exchange during a Friday afternoon selloff. It was jammed with fed-up holiday travelers; trains were running late, and tempers were running high.

Then, just as advertised, a small, plump, pale, dark-haired girl materialized. She was pretty, in a frowsy, chaotically put-together way. She wore a navy blue pea coat and a little too much lipstick, and she looked to be in her early to mid twenties. More to the point, she didn't look like a fed. "Are you Peter?" she asked. "God, you are really tall. What are you, seven feet or something?"

"Six six."

"So . . ."

"So . . ." I said brilliantly. "So, the Beatles," I went on, as if I were in a hurry, as though Penn Station was the first of many Friday night stops.

The girl extracted a shiny, black plastic drawstring bag

from her purse, which she handed over with great delicacy. The bag was heavy and splitting a little along the sides. "Here, you can go ahead and check on everything if you want."

"It's OK," I said. "I trust you." I took out my wallet and began counting off bills, ignoring the well-known adage never to flash money in a public space. Was anybody eyeballing us? "You said a hundred and ten, right?"

"Right." She took the money without counting it, stuffing the bills into her coat pocket. "Thanks."

"No, hey, listen, thank you."

"Look inside the bag. You told me he was seven, right?" I nodded. "There's a couple of extra little things in there for him. Go ahead, look."

Folded atop a clump of half a dozen professional-looking CDs was a faded blue rag, which, when I pulled it out, revealed itself to be a worn-out child-size T-shirt with a single word—*HELP!*—stenciled in black capitals across the front.

"That used to be mine," the girl explained hurriedly. "It doesn't fit me anymore, obviously. It was one of my first Beatles T-shirts ever. I know it's kind of ratty, but it's kind of great, too. I thought your son might like it. It's clean," she added hastily. "I washed it."

"Thank you—" but she interrupted me.

"There's also a Sgt. Pepper mouse pad in there. I thought your little boy might like that, too. I have a couple of them." She took a deep breath. "Can I just say I think it's so cool that a seven-year-old kid loves the Beatles? It just made me feel so happy when you told me that! It's like now I know for sure their music will go on forever. Which I knew it would anyway, but still?" She checked, or pretended to check, her watch. "Anyhow, you can e-mail me if you ever need to order more stuff. So . . . g'bye then. So long."

She turned, raising one hand in the air, and wriggled her fingertips once, in an imitation of unabashed cosmopolitan assurance. Then she was gone.

The second I got home, I showed the bootlegs to Maggie, and later that night, when Sam was asleep, I played one up in my office. The songs were bizarrely unfamiliar. A medley of "Sausages and French Fries," "Early in the Morning," and "Hi-Ho Silver"? What was that all about? How about "She Came in through the Bathroom Window" mixed with "Baa Baa Black Sheep"? What about "Blue Suede Shoes" followed by "Hava Nagila"? Sam, I knew, would be over the moon. *I* was over the moon.

Then there was the battered T-shirt Billy had tucked into the bag. It was too small for Sam, but Billy's desire to pass on some of the happiness she got from the Beatles to a new boy put a lump in the back of my throat.

On Christmas morning, I got up early, crept downstairs into the living room, and after peering out the window to see if it was snowing—it never is, when you want it to—I plugged in the tree lights and started the coffee. When it was done, I brought two cups upstairs, one for Maggie. "Did you remember to eat some of that carrot the kids left out for the reindeer?" she murmured.

No. Back downstairs, a single crunch, making sure to

leave tooth marks. The children had also left Santa a glass of orange juice, so I took a swig of that, too.

A half-hour later, the kids tumbled downstairs.

Of the three children, Sam has always been the most patient, philosophical present opener. He carefully unwraps something, removes what's inside, then immediately begins to build it, inflate it, read it, roll it, play it, or try it on. I admired this withholding quality — wished I had it myself — but it also slowed things down, and as the morning crept toward eleven and he still hadn't gotten to the bootlegs, I seized the package from under the tree and knelt down next to him on the rug.

"Sam," I said, man-to-man. "Here's a little something. It's not from Santa Claus, actually, it's from me."

This was a strange distinction to make. But selfishly, I didn't want Santa Claus to get credit for something that I'd knocked myself out to get. Who'd done all the legwork, Santa or me? Who'd dragged himself down to Penn Station, Santa or me? Huh? I handed over the bootlegs. "Merry Christmas," I said.

The first disk he pulled out was *The Complete Rooftop Concert*. He stared at it for a moment without understanding. His mind, I guessed, was whirring: *But wait a minute, I have everything the Beatles ever recorded. But—* He then gazed at me with a nearly helpless happiness. "Dad, what *are* these?"

"They're bootlegs," I said suavely. I explained the concept to him — engineers, sound technicians, and even producers pocketing master tapes, then releasing them to collectors and radio stations, or else people secretly taping stadium concerts, or practice sessions recorded but never released, or old radio broadcasts discovered under a yellowing wedding dress or a broken hair dryer in a Cornwall shed.

"But where did you *get* them?" Sam asked.

I shrugged, I hoped mysteriously.

I scarfed down a quick breakfast, and when I came back to the living room, Sam was gone, leaving a pile of presents unopened under the tree. "I think he's gone off somewhere with his bootlegs," Maggie commented, and distantly, clashing rudely with the sound of Nat King Cole and his chestnuts, I could make out the middle eight section of "Don't Let Me Down" floating down the stairwell. Eventually, I coaxed Sam downstairs to finish opening his other presents. But by five in the afternoon he was back upstairs in his bedroom, glued to the bootlegs.

"Dad," he said when I came in later to say good night. "Hear this."

He aimed his remote and clicked. A reggae version of "Ob-La-Di, Ob-La-Da" was playing, but now it switched over to a version of "Oh! Darling," with Paul singing falsetto in the bridge, and John joining in for the last chorus. In an interview, Sam told me now, John had said that Paul didn't sing the song as well as he, John, could have. "I think I still like Paul's version the best," Sam added politely.

His voice went on, halting, light. Basically he was concerned that if bootlegs were illegal, then the Beatles wouldn't see any money from them, and that wasn't right. He loved listening to the bootlegs. He was happy to own them. He was amazed that they even existed. It was really nice of me, and all that. But he was frankly worried about how the Beatles might react. "If I ever met Paul someday," he said, "and I'm not saying I'm ever *going* to meet Paul. But if I did"—he shook his head—"I just really don't know what I would say to him."

Torn between pride and a faint panic that his integrity would keep him from playing the bootlegs, I hurriedly explained that illegal recordings were an integral part of the music industry (they were, weren't they?) and that some groups, the Grateful Dead, for example, actually encouraged their fans to make tapes of their concerts. That in some ways, bootlegs encouraged consumers to buy the actual, commercially released records. "And it's nice of you to be concerned about the Beatles not seeing any money," I said, "but you should know they're all pretty much set, financially."

This seemed to mollify Sam somewhat. We sat in silence for a moment. "There's something called the spirit of the law versus the letter of the law," I explained. "The letter says, 'This is the law. I expect you to follow it literally, exactly.' The spirit of the law basically says, 'We make laws to serve us, not so we can be ruled by them. Let *us* decide what's right or wrong.' Just so you know, I would never do something to rip off the Beatles. They deserve every bit of money they have. In fact, I think the Beatles deserve *more* money than they have. Back to bootlegs. Yeah, it's illegal to have them and own them. But shouldn't you and I decide if we want to take that risk?"

"Wait," Sam said, a little confused by this dumbed-down guide to the legal system, "so it's my choice."

"I want you to decide if you think bootlegs should be illegal. Because if you do"—my heart fell a little—"I can give them away. Or, I don't know, use them as drink coasters."

He pondered this, all the while fingering the plastic shells of his bootlegs. "I think I like the spirit of the law," he said at last. "That's the one that lets you listen to the bootlegs, right?"

"Right."

"The spirit then."

It was final. Sam seemed relieved and, a moment later, reinvigorated. "So, Dad, what do you want to hear?"

I didn't even have to think about it. "I want to hear the medley of 'Blue Suede Shoes' and 'Hava Nagila.'"

5.
The
White
Album

ANY PREOCCUPATION with the Beatles invariably rams up against a few difficult, R-rated subjects. Drugs. Death. A lot of death, actually. Death by natural causes, by illness, by suicide, by speeding car, by assassin, by hoax. A cheerfully sinister darkness—the darkness of carnivals, Ouija boards, and Venetian masks—always underscored the Beatles' legacy. A second grader could pick up on it, and quickly mine did.

Drugs drew his attention first. Having read in one of his books that "Lucy in the Sky with Diamonds" was an anagram for LSD and that LSD was a drug, Sam asked me one day if it was true the Beatles "ever did that kind of stuff."

I was almost relieved the subject had come up. We'd skirted it once or twice already, and I wasn't thrilled with how I'd handled it. When I'd brought home the video of

"Magical Mystery Tour" and screened it for the kids one night, Sam inquired, "Why do Paul's eyes look so funny?"

Without thinking, I said, "He's probably stoned."

Nice. I waited tensely, hoping my words would drop gently into the pillows of the couch and stay buried there. Miraculously, they did. Now I resolved to face the subject head-on. I explained that LSD was a drug popular in the 1960s and that "stoned" was like "drunk." Drugs, I went on, were things people smoked, swallowed, snorted, and injected. They could make you feel either great or down in the dumps. Many of them, I emphasized, were illegal. "In the 1960s, a lot of people experimented with different things," I explained. "Drugs included. A lot of artists thought drugs could help them write better or perform better or be better people. And the Beatles were certainly part of that time."

"Oh." Sam looked confused. "So they *did*, right?"

"Yes, but most people their age were trying out different things."

"Have *you* ever tried drugs?"

Um. "I'd be lying if I said I haven't tried a drug or two," I said, "but I didn't really like the feeling. In the end, it's kind of a waste of time."

Sam digested this. "So the letter of the law says you can't. And the spirit of the law says you can't stop me."

"Right," I said. "And the Beatles chose—"

"The spirit."

"Big-time," I concluded.

• • •

Death was a more complex, far-reaching subject. It also wouldn't go away. After all, references to death or dying showed up in countless songs: "Eleanor Rigby," "Maxwell's Silver Hammer," "In My Life," "Good Morning," "She Said She Said," "A Day in the Life."

Even if you overlooked the music, then there were the real-life deaths. Early on, I'd reluctantly told Sam that a deranged man gunned down John Lennon outside his Manhattan apartment building. And one day, when Sam asked Maggie and me to go over the Beatles chronology, from Liverpool to the breakup, I was surprised by how often we stumbled onto people dying: thirty-two-year-old Brian Epstein, the suave, tormented manager of the Beatles responsible for smoothing out their ruffian roots, dead of a drug overdose in his London apartment. Bassist Stuart Sutcliffe, an early member of the group, dead at age twenty-two of a cerebral hemorrhage. Paul's mother, Mary, dead of breast cancer at age forty-two, when her son was only fourteen, and two years after that, John's mother, Julia, hit and killed by a car driven by a drunken Liverpool cop.

"John was living with his aunt Mimi at the time," I told Sam. "Julia had just come back into John's life, and he adored her. It was late at night, and Julia was walking back to the bus station. John heard the screech, and then the crash."

At first Sam's questions about death were general: Who was Eleanor Rigby, and why didn't anybody go to her funeral? Did the guy in "Maxwell's Silver Hammer" really go around hitting people on the head? Why? Then, with any child's fascination with morbidity, these evolved into more pointed questions: What did dying feel like? Is there a Heaven? What about Hell? Who was the first person I knew who died? When John was killed, what happened to his body afterward?

"The strange thing is that it was Paul, and not John, who a lot of people assumed was dead," I informed Sam one day. This was a minor cop-out, a sidestep away from a topic that threatened to become too heavy too soon. "There was a rumor going around in the late 1960s that Paul had died and that the other Beatles had replaced him with an imposter, then hushed it up because they didn't want the world to know."

Sam perked up. "Oh yeah," he said slowly. "I *read* something about that."

The Paul-is-dead phenomenon got under way in the winter of 1969 when, in response to information given by a mysterious phone caller who gave his name only as "Tom," a Michigan radio station broadcast a bulletin that Paul McCartney had been killed in a car accident three years earlier. Shortly thereafter, a University of Michigan student named Fred LaBour expanded on the Paul-is-dead thesis in a quasi-satirical article in the *Michigan Daily.* The story went like this: Leaving Apple Studios in November 1966, after an all-night recording session during which he'd quarreled with John Lennon, Paul apparently sped back home in a rainstorm to his house in St. John's Wood in North London. It was early morning, midweek. Paul was behind the wheel of his Aston Martin. Some reports placed a woman in the passenger seat, doing her best to distract him; others speculated the woman in question was a meter maid (*Took her home / we nearly made it*). In any event, Paul skidded through a red light, was blindsided by another car, and died. Some people even speculated that the cutest Beatle of all was decapitated.

News services picked up the story and ran with it. "Paul is dead!" someone shouted at Johnny Carson during his *Tonight Show* monologue. According to Beatles theorists, Paul's death was immediately hushed up. Why risk putting a shock ending to a musical machine such as the Beatles? Imagine the sums of money that would be lost, the fans who would drop away. Huddling with unnamed advisors, the three remaining Beatles came up with a bizarre, risky, and somewhat labored solution: they would replace Paul with a look-alike, a small-time actor named William Campbell, who'd won a Paul McCartney look-alike contest in his hometown of Edinburgh. Better yet for keeping the story under wraps, Campbell was an orphan, and thus untraceable. The public would be none the worse for not knowing. The Beatles could carry on as they always had. Since Campbell—who may have also gone by the pseudonym "Billy Shears"—was two or three inches taller than the real Paul, this neatly explained why the Beatles had stopped appearing live after their 1966 Candlestick Park concert.

And yet the surviving three felt guilty about the ruse. Conflicted. Evidently, John felt the worst. If he hadn't quarreled with Paul that night, the accident would never have happened. In any case, the three Beatles began to attach coded messages to songs, and to album-cover artwork, as an indirect way of alerting Beatles fans across the world that, yes, Paul was gone.

"Wait, I can see why the other three Beatles would feel bad, but why would they feel guilty?"

I wasn't entirely sure. Was this how most people's guilt played out? Of course, logic had never played a significant role in the Paul-is-dead phenomenon. You simply accepted the premise and ran with it. I pulled out Sam's cracked *Abbey Road* CD. "I'll show you a famous clue. See this little Volkswagen bug on the cover?"

"Uh-huh."

"Look what the license plate says."

"Twenty-eight-I-F," Sam recited.

"No. It's twenty-eight *IF*. See, the way the story goes, Paul would've been twenty-eight *if* he'd lived . . ."

Sam studied the cover. "No, he wouldn't," he said at last.

"Yeah, I think he would have been."

"Dad, no, he would've been *twenty-seven*." Sam went over to the bookcase to check one of his several Beatles trivia books. He flipped through the pages, then let out a small exhalation of triumph. Just as he'd thought: Paul was born on June 22, 1942, and *Abbey Road* was released in September of 1969. Paul would have turned twenty-seven the previous June, right? "That's not a very good clue at all," Sam concluded cheerfully.

Oh. "Then here's another." Still holding up *Abbey Road*, I pointed out how, walking together, the Beatles comprised an informal funeral procession. George, with his denim shirt tucked into skintight jeans, was assumed to be the gravedigger. Paul, barefoot, in formal black, and out of step with the others, was the corpse. ("Remember, also, that the real Paul is left-handed. So here's something to think about: Why is Paul holding his cigarette in his *right* hand?") Ringo, striding just ahead of Paul, is the undertaker, and John, dressed all in white, is supposed to represent a deity, maybe Jesus himself.

I hadn't thought about the Paul-is-dead affair in decades. But now, starting off with *Abbey Road,* Sam and I spent the rest of the afternoon poring over Beatles album covers and studying the most famous clues. Why (I asked Sam) were the yellow hyacinths covering the gravesite on the cover of *Sgt. Pepper* shaped like a left-handed guitar? Why did the hyacinths appear to spell out the word "Paul"? ("I don't see that," Sam broke in. "It looks like maybe it spells 'rub.' Or 'grub.'") Why, on the *Sgt. Pepper* cover, was someone holding a lone raised hand over Paul's head, supposedly a symbol of death or benediction in certain Far Eastern religions?

"What do you mean, Far Eastern religions?" Sam asked. Clearly he'd decided to play devil's advocate here.

"Uh, certain ones," I said vaguely. "I'm not altogether sure which."

He wouldn't let up. "Dad, *which Far Eastern religions?*"

"Certain ones!" I repeated, and pushed onward. How about the dots on the back of *Abbey Road* that seemed to form a numeral "3," as if to inform the world that where once there were four Beatles, there were now only three? Why had the band decided, midway through their career, to drop the "The" and refer to themselves simply as "Beatles"?

"Were they telling the world they were a different group now?" I asked Sam.

He stared at me. "Or, Dad," he said finally, with a little laugh, "is it just because . . . you're making all this stuff up?"

I had to admit: more than thirty-five years since it first obsessed and terrified me, the whole Paul-is-dead controversy seemed ridiculous, a paranoid Rorschach for a hysterically overinvolved fan base. But in the late 1960s such speculations were taken seriously, not only by eight-year-old boys like me, but by millions of fans and major media. Lawyer F. Lee Bailey hosted a network TV special that I watched with my parents, devoted to uncovering and studying album-cover clues. *Life* magazine ran a cover story titled "Paul Is Still with Us" that ended up suggesting the opposite to some. The magazine had positioned a car advertisement directly behind a photo of Paul; when you held the page up to the light, the car appeared to chop Paul's head off.

I was a suggestible kid. There were nights I could hardly sleep I was so unnerved by the thought of Paul's dying. At the same time, I savored its delectable horror: the corpse on the slick road, the ruined car, the incredulous crowd. Over and over again, I replayed the final few seconds of "Strawberry Fields Forever," where I heard John's lugubrious voice intoning "*I buried Paul.*" (John later explained that he often uttered silly phrases during long recording sessions; that time he'd said, "cranberry sauce.") I resented my parents for not owning a record player that could play Beatles songs backward, such as "I'm So Tired," which evidently yielded

"*Paul's dead, man, miss him, miss him,*" and the dreaded "Revolution 9," in which it was said listeners could make out a garbled "*Turn me on, dead man.*"

The fear that Paul was dead, and that the other Beatles had concealed it, briefly took over my life. It made the rest of the world seem treacherous and unstable. If the Beatles wore such a false face, then what else was bogus? What other truths were hidden from me? Was I adopted?

I wanted Sam to understand my murky childhood mindset, and at the same time, I didn't. Who would wish fear and dread on an eight-year-old? Then I realized I'd never really talked to anybody about Paul's "death," not at the time, not since then. My parents and my sister, I remember, didn't believe a word of it. Most people I've met over the years claimed they'd dismissed the whole thing from the start. "You actually believed that?" they asked me. It was a pleasure — and a relief — to rehash it with Sam.

To him, the Paul-is-dead scenario was morbid fun, but no different, really, from *Where's Waldo?* or his *I Spy* books. The idea of Paul dying and being replaced by an imposter strained credulity, to say the least. It would mean, among other things, that the letter and doodle framed above Sam's bed was counterfeit. Over the next few months, we made a game of it, me playing the believer, Sam the bubble-puncturing skeptic. Not for the first time, I realized this game reversed our usual roles. Now I was the avid seeker of Beatles-related insight, and Sam was the expert, patiently dipping into his vast trove of Beatles knowledge, helping me separate truth from misperception, logic from paranoiac fancy. "Just *suppose,* Sam," I kept saying. "Just *suppose* some brilliant plastic surgeon changed William Campbell's face around so that he looked exactly like Paul. I mean, *what if?*"

"OK, OK, Dad. Even if somebody did replace Paul, that doesn't mean that person would *sound* like Paul."

"What about vocal surgery?"

"What's vocal surgery?"

"Like a whole new set of vocal cords and throat muscles. A brand new larynx."

"Dad, I don't think there even *is* vocal surgery—"

"There probably isn't, but—"

"OK, Dad, what about *songs?* How could some guy named William Campbell write Paul McCartney songs? It doesn't make any sense. *Think* about it."

Despite his skepticism, I hadn't seen Sam so excited about the Beatles since he'd first heard *Abbey Road.* Despite an occasional time-out, his interest in the group was still all-encompassing. Over the past year, he'd listened repeatedly to every single Beatles record. He'd watched every single Beatles film countless times. Now, impelled by the possibility that he'd been denied certain crucial information, he embarked on a terrier-like reappraisal of Beatles music. The next few weekends he spent holed up in his room, sleuthing with a magnifying glass and headphones. Sometimes he would bring the magnifying glass to meals, where it took up position next to his knife and fork. Beatles music seeped out from under the door nearly continuously. Then, he would come shooting into my office or bedroom with a bulletin. Did I remember how in "Come Together," John sang, "One and one and one is three"? Was *that* a Paul-is-dead clue? What about the song "Hello, Goodbye"? Was Paul telling us "good-bye" while William Campbell was saying "hello"?

A scrupulous investigation of Paul-is-dead songs and album-cover clues led Sam, inevitably, to *The White Album,* which he now began to play in earnest. Except for "Revolution 9" and "Why Don't We Do It in the Road?" he adored *The White Album,* and was puzzled to find I didn't share his enthusiasm for it. "Dad," he said to me, "it's the Beatles' best album. Or at least a lot of people think that. Why don't you like it?"

"I *do* like parts of it," and I did: "While My Guitar Gently Weeps," "Yer Blues," "Happiness Is a Warm Gun," and a few others.

I explained to Sam that when I was his age, "It wasn't an easy time. The Vietnam War was going on. Richard Nixon was president. There were riots in American cities. Good people were being assassinated. I associated *The White Album* with all this rotten stuff going on in the world." Sam didn't understand, so I explained further. "Music can remind you of great times, or it can remind you of times you wouldn't mind forgetting. Back then was the first time I realized the world could be a nasty place."

"Like it is now?"

"Yeah, a lot like it is now."

Silently, Sam took this in. "Dad, you shouldn't blame *The White Album,*" he said softly at last. "It's not *The White Album*'s fault."

From then on, he made it a priority to reintroduce me to

the album. Or to cheerfully torment me with it, I wasn't sure which. He put it on first thing in the morning, as he was getting ready for school. "I like playing 'Back in the U.S.S.R.' when I get up," he announced. "Or 'Birthday.' It makes me get dressed more quickly." Sometimes he'd call out, "Dad, can you come here for a second?" and when I'd come into his bedroom, Sam would be sitting on his bed with "Savoy Truffle" blaring from his tape recorder. "Dad," he'd say, sounding perplexed. "I can't *believe* you don't like this song. This song is about *chocolates*!"

Ultimately, a fake death — Paul's — took us right back to a real-life death: John's. His favorite songs on *The White Album* all contained Lennon vocals, and his growing admiration for John as a musician brought us back to the subject of his murder. Sam began peppering me with questions about John's life in New York City. Did he walk around on the streets? Was he surrounded by bodyguards? Did he wear disguises? Watching *Imagine*, a documentary about John's life and death, had softened his feelings about the Lennon family, particularly when he found out that John took a musical sabbatical in the late 1970s in order to take care of his young son.

Sean Lennon riveted Sam. Part of it was his sheer adorableness, and part was the intuitive empathy children often feel toward one another. "Was Sean really sad when John died?" Sam asked me repeatedly.

"Sean was really, really young at the time — he was five, younger than you are — but yeah, I'm sure it made him really sad. To grow up without a father around. I'm sure he missed his dad terribly." I couldn't believe I was saying this, me, who'd once deemed fathers useless.

"Was Paul sad when John died?"

"I'm sure he was," I said, adding that when a journalist asked Paul to comment about John's murder, Paul threw out, "It's a drag," before slipping inside a waiting car. "I don't think Paul meant that at all," I went on. "I don't think Paul was thinking well that day. Sometimes people say things they don't mean when they feel really bad, and they regret them afterward. I'll bet Paul was in shock that day. Absolutely stunned. Not to mention scared that somebody might take a shot at him, too."

The next day, when Sam came home from school, I brought him upstairs to listen to a song off Paul McCartney's solo album *Tug of War*. "Paul wrote this song about John," I explained, "seven years after John died."

In "Here Today," Paul imagines what he would say to John if he were alive. John, he suspects, would laugh at him if Paul dared to claim that the two of them knew each other well. John would say, the lyric went on, that the two were "worlds apart." "I'm holding back the tears no more," Paul sings, adding, "I love you."

I was seated in my office armchair, with Sam perched on the thick sidearm, leaning into me. When I glanced up at my son, he was biting down on his lower lip; he looked like he was going to cry. "What?" I asked softly.

"It's just really, really sad to me that John died, that's all."

"I know, Sam. I think about it a lot."

"I do, too."

"Do you?"

"Yeah. It's so *stupid.* That it happened, I mean."

Stupid, like *jerk* or *idiot* or *shut up,* was one of those words I discouraged my children from using. "That's the perfect word for it," I said now.

Sam asked me to play "Here Today" again. "So what do you think John would say to Paul if he were alive?" I asked Sam as the song ended a second time.

No hesitation. "I don't know. Maybe 'I love you, too'?" And then Sam asked if we could ever visit the Dakota.

"This is it," I said as we approached the gloomy, ornate apartment complex on the corner of West Seventy-second Street and Central Park West in Manhattan.

I'd had my reservations about taking Sam here. It felt prurient. Any visit to the Dakota, after all, is a visit to a murder scene. But Sam had insisted he wanted to see where John Lennon had spent the last few years of his life—where he hung out with Sean and Yoko. Framed in this everyday manner, I agreed to take him one Saturday afternoon. Built across from Central Park in 1882, the Dakota got its name from being so far removed from New York City's other buildings. Recently cleaned and refurbished on the outside, it still oozes architectural malevolence. Roman Polanski's *Rosemary's Baby* was filmed here. On the sunniest day, it looks like a huge, sulking bully. The apartments inside are high ceilinged, the windows imposingly broad. A passerby can spot signs of the frayed yet expensive life within—a huge sailboat model; a lamp with a yellowing shade, dilapidated curtains. Yoko Ono still lives here in several adjoining apartments on a high floor.

As we approached the Dakota, Sam skipped ahead, and I caught up with him outside a glassed-in booth. I nodded at a doorman reading the *Daily News*. Long accustomed to peering, scurrying passersby, he barely looked up, even when a cluster of Japanese tourists appeared with their Nikons, followed by a European couple with a video camera. Few people, I noticed, were able to pass by the entrance without taking a furtive peek into the courtyard, though it might have been more an instinctive fascination with wealth than with the site where John Lennon met his end.

Since there wasn't a whole lot else to do — we couldn't go inside, after all — Sam and I took up positions on the stone wall bordering Central Park. "It looks like such a depressing place," Sam said finally.

"Yoko lives way high up," I remarked, pointing. "She might be up there right now. Sean, too."

"Do you think they're looking at us?"

"I don't know, Sam. What's your guess?"

He waved. "Hi, Yoko. Hi, Sean."

Every year, I told Sam, fans gathered on the sidewalk on the eighth of December, the anniversary of John's 1980 death. Some brought boom boxes, others candles, lighters, albums. "People need a place to go," I explained. "An actual physical *place* to pay tribute to a dead person. And when someone dies, you want to be with other people who really care about that person."

Two of Us

I hadn't told Sam much about John's murder. Nearly twenty-five years after it happened, I still had no trouble hating the man who did it. In general, I found murderers fairly interesting, but I had no desire to read about this one or talk about him or know more than I did already. Over the years I'd convinced myself that if I said his name aloud, he would have achieved precisely what he wanted, which was fame. When Sam asked, I mumbled his name once, hurriedly. It hardly mattered what his name was.

Now I told Sam that there were Beatles fans who weren't right in the head. "There was a guy named Charles Manson who thought the Beatles were trying to communicate with him personally. That they were sending messages to him. "He heard the line 'I'm in love but I'm lazy' in 'Honey Pie' and thought this meant the Beatles loved him but that they were depending on Manson to make the first move. Take the song 'Blackbird,'" I went on. "What does that song make you think of?"

"Birds," Sam said, adding eagerly, "but, Dad, that song wasn't really about birds. Paul wrote it during the Civil Rights movement. It's about black people." He hesitated. "And, like, 'bird' means woman or something, if you're from England?"

"OK," I said. "But Charles Manson heard that song and thought, 'The Beatles are trying to communicate with me through this song. They're telling me it's time for an uprising by African-Americans. And that the Beatles are calling that uprising 'Helter Skelter.'"

"But, Dad, that's *crazy.*"

"Tell me about it."

"'Helter Skelter' was a *carnival* ride," Sam said. "God, what was this guy's problem?" His voice sounded braver than I think he felt.

"I don't know. But Charles Manson heard in that song what he wanted to hear." I hesitated. "Anyhow, the guy shot John several times. John was rushed to a hospital near here, on Fifty-ninth Street, and the doctors tried to save his life, but they couldn't." I turned to Sam. "The whole thing still makes me so angry. I can still remember exactly where I was when it happened. Most people in their thirties and forties can."

I was in New York, I told him, in my junior year of college. My roommate told me that a deranged fan had shot John Lennon. An hour later, Lennon was declared dead.

"At times like that, you freeze," I said. "You remember everything about where you are, and what you're doing." For me, it was a narrow living room, a gray-white rug, a sober newscaster; the fire escape outside my window; the dislocating, disbelieving drift that followed when "wounded" turned into "dead."

Sam's mother, I went on, happened to be living in New York at the time, too, though we didn't know each other yet. She went down to the Dakota that night to pay her respects. "As I said, you just"—how to put it?—"needed to be with other people that night."

"Mom was here that night?"

"Uh-huh."

"Wow. She never told me that." He appeared to be pondering adults, their mystery.

We padded down into the small, enclosed chunk of Central Park known as Strawberry Fields and took seats on a bench opposite the paved memorial that reads "Imagine." I explained to Sam that the real Strawberry Field (no *s* attached) was an orphanage in Liverpool, but that after John's death, Yoko Ono transformed this portion of Central Park into a tribute to her husband.

We sat on the bench for a while. "I would've really loved to see John Lennon get older," I said after a while. "Mellow out a bit. Write new stuff. Remember, there were only four people in the world who really knew what it was like to be a Beatle. I always think about what John might have become. What he might have done with the rest of his life."

"Yeah, I know," Sam said. He sighed.

Across from us, an old hippie with a guitar was singing a broken-voiced version of George Harrison's "All Things Must Pass."

"Dad?" Sam broke in suddenly.

"Uh-huh?"

"What does 'All Things Must Pass' mean?"

He'd listened repeatedly to George Harrison's mammoth, three-record set. He could hum the songs and pick them out on the piano. But as I'd learned a few times before, that didn't always mean he understood what the lyrics meant.

"It's a euphemism for dying," I explained after a moment.

"What's a 'euphemism'?"

"It's a polite way of saying something that's hard to say. I prefer 'dying' myself. Because death is a part of life. There's no need to sugarcoat it. What are you going to say, that

John Lennon 'passed away'? It sounds pretty and all, but it's false. He died violently.

"After John died," I went on, "people started thinking and writing about him as if he were a saint, or a prophet. That happens sometimes when a great musician dies young. But I don't think that's a good idea. From what I've read, John was a very complicated guy. I doubt he was a saint. And I don't think he would have wanted to be remembered as one, either."

"Did you come down to the Dakota that night, too?"

"No, I stayed at home and watched TV." I hesitated. "My father actually called me the next day about it."

The Beatles had long since ceased to play much of a role in either my life or my father's, but he must have remembered the music from our long childhood summers, and I knew that reports about John's death were dominating the news. We chatted about the usual things—how classes were going, what the dog was up to, the weather. Then he paused a moment and said that he "just wanted to check in."

"I'm sorry," he went on with difficulty, "about what happened to your Beatle friend. It's a crazy world out there sometimes." And then we said our good-byes.

"Your dad *called* you when John Lennon died?" Sam said.

"Uh-huh. I think it was his way of telling me he loved me, and was thinking of me, actually."

"I can't believe your dad called you," Sam said, shaking his head. "I thought you said he was kind of shy."

"He was a lot of things," I said. "He had a great laugh, a great sense of humor, a lot of verve. You would've loved him, Sam. He was a very emotional man. But sometimes it was hard for him to show it."

"But then *he* died, too," Sam went on in a rapt voice. Then, "Were you really sad when your dad died?"

"Yeah, I was."

"How old were you?"

"I was around thirty." By then, I told Sam, my father had retired from teaching, and was sick and getting sicker. He'd given up smoking years earlier, but the cigarettes had done what they were supposed to do. More and more, I was struck by his fragility, by the bags under his eyes, by his long naps and early bedtimes, and how even during cool New England days he needed the air conditioner going to counteract the suffocation of emphysema.

There probably comes a moment in every son's life when he realizes he's physically stronger than his father. That moment came for me when we were shaking hands good-bye at the train station after one of those weekends home — despite the sudden drowner's urgency I felt in his grip, his hand was weak. Afterward I cried on the train going back to New York. He died a year later.

"You cried?" Sam asked.

I had the impression that the way I answered him would either give him permission, or not, to cry himself in the future.

"Yeah, I did. Grownups cry," I said. "Men, women. Not just children. You'd be surprised. But you know something? Death is OK. Death is *supposed* to happen."

"I think I'll cry a lot when you die," Sam said after a moment.

"Hold on, don't kill me off yet."

"Dad, I'm not. I'm talking about *later.*"

"Well, I know I'd cry if you died, too. I'd be a wreck."
Just thinking about it put tears in my eyes.

Death kept weighing on Sam's mind. He'd seen the photographs of Linda McCartney horseback riding in the weeks before she died, and he shared my indignation at the media at publishing a map of the McCartney ranch in Arizona.

"I think Mom is really sad," he told me on the night of Linda's death. She was, too. I found her in front of the computer, searching for Linda news on the Internet. "Poor Paul," Maggie said. "Linda seemed like such a good egg."

That night, in the kitchen, the conversation kept circling back to Linda. "Do you know why I liked her so much?" Maggie said at one point. "I mean, I don't even know this person, but still . . . it's because she had next to no interest in living this glamorous, nightclubbing, swishy life. She protected her kids, sent them to normal schools, and put aside her career for her family. It's just like Jackie Onassis said: If you don't do a good job raising your children, I don't think whatever else you do well matters very much."

All three kids were sitting around the kitchen table. Five feet away, Maggie flicked the oven knob; whirred salad leaves in the spinner; clattered forks and spoons onto plates. Her blond hair flopped around her shoulders. Her long-standing admiration for Linda had always puzzled me slightly, and I liked teasing her about it. She didn't mind. Once, she explained that when she, Maggie, was young,

Linda seemed an antidote to the brasher forms of feminism then sweeping the country. She had a career, but gave it up to raise her kids.

And Maggie's own life? A graduate of a top-notch college. Two graduate degrees. A Harvard fellowship. A private therapy practice. All of which she tossed aside when Sam was born. Of course women can have it all, Maggie liked to say. Except that someone has to suffer, and usually it'll be the kids. At the risk of being reductive, I saw, suddenly, that Linda hadn't only been my wife's teenage role model, but a longer-lasting one.

Then, of course, there was George Harrison. In the late 1990s, doctors had diagnosed him with throat cancer. The disease eventually spread into his lungs and brain. A tumor. Inoperable. It appeared that the 1998 incident in which a schizophrenic fan broke into George's house and stabbed him repeatedly in the chest had inflamed a condition brought on by a lifetime of smoking.

Since learning about George's condition, Sam had been on an informal deathwatch. Every morning before school, he'd asked us, "So . . . any new news about George?" There was rarely anything to report. Or rather, the reports flowing in from England were various, carefully worded. George was feeling fine. He appreciated the world's concern, prayers, good wishes. Things were looking up. He was receiving the best medical care possible. And then came silence. Weeks went by, a month, then several. Followed by new, flimsy hearsay: George didn't have much time left. Specialists in London, Minnesota, and even Staten Island were treating him. He'd recorded a final track with bandleader

Jools Holland, assigning the songwriting copyright to R.I.P. Productions, Inc. Perhaps there was material enough for a final album. Maybe it would be called "Brainwashed," maybe something else. And where was George, anyway? Maybe in Los Angeles. Maybe in Hawaii. Maybe holed up in England. Maybe Paul and Ringo had spent an emotional few hours at his bedside, saying good-bye; maybe they hadn't.

One afternoon, as Sam and I tossed a Frisbee in the backyard, he commented, with seeming offhandedness, "So Mom said that George isn't doing too well."

"Yeah, I know."

"Do you think that he's going to die soon?"

"I don't know, Sam. It's serious, what he has."

"He has what your dad, right?"

"Kind of," I said. "They're both caused by smoking."

"Dad?"

"Uh-huh?"

"You remember you asked me once why I liked George the best of the Beatles?"

"Uh-huh."

He'd never put it into words before, but now he tried. "I think it's because I like *seconds*. People who are *second*. John and Paul, they were like the number one Beatles, but George was the *second*. I always liked the way George looked. He had the coolest guitar on the roof, too. The black and white one." Sam was referring to the rooftop concert at the end of the film *Let It Be*. "I guess he reminds me of me a little bit."

"In what way?"

"Just . . . he's quiet, that's all." Another beat. "He always seems to be thinking about things." A shrug. "I don't know."

The bad news reached us on a gray November afternoon.

A phone call from a friend, confirmation on the Internet, and then I went into the living room to turn on CNN. George's death was the lead story. Practically every news station was showing old black-and-white clips not just of George but of all the Beatles. They beamed and waved as they descended the stairs from an airplane; they shot back answers at reporters during an early-1960s press conference; they took their bows in unison, four boys in collarless jackets. Their cheeks were unlined, their hair shaggy, their tongues sharp; they seemed cutting and naïve at the same time. In most of the clips, I noticed that George had a cigarette going.

Eventually, Maggie joined me on the couch. "God, it's just so sad," she said. "I don't know why. He had a fantastic life. But it just . . ."

George's death, Maggie went on, didn't have the shock effect of John's, but it felt more final somehow. It wasn't that she held out any hope or desire for the Beatles to get back together. That would be a mistake. She recalled the fan who once asked John Lennon if the Beatles were ever going to reunite. And his fast response: "When are you going back to high school?"

It was more the principle of the thing. People kept unconscious maps in their heads, a topography of friends, places, even celebrities that reassured you that things were right, or at least OK, in the world. When someone like George Harrison died, you realized: *George was on my map.* Now the map had been shrunk, redrawn. Paul, busy as ever, and Ringo, somewhere in the south of France, were the only Beatles left now.

Sam was due back from school in a couple of hours, and I started rehearsing how I would break the news to him.

He knew already, though. He'd overheard a couple of teachers talking about it during lunch. His sisters knew, too; he'd told them at pickup.

"I'm not surprised," Sam said now as he tossed his small, orange backpack in the front hall. He didn't sound glum, just tired.

"What are you not surprised about?" I asked.

"It just . . . wasn't looking very good for him, was it?"

A flash of adulthood rose, then dove back down. "No," I said, "it wasn't." I got up and hugged him. "Sorry, Sam."

"It's OK." Sam stood uncertainly in the living room doorway. "I feel sorriest of all for his family. His son and everybody."

He went upstairs to do his homework, the unserious kind teachers give second graders. He liked to get it done first thing so he could hang out with his family later. For a while, the house was silent except for the recapitulations of George's death. CNN. C-Span. MSNBC. VH1. MTV. Even the local news. A half-hour later, Sam reappeared in the living room. "I don't really feel like doing my homework now," he said.

"Can I get you anything?"

"Are there any Reese's Peanut Butter Cups?" Recently, Sam and I had discovered that Reese's were our favorite chocolate.

I fetched a couple from the kitchen, and for the next several minutes, Sam and I watched a clip of George from a late-1980s talk show. "God, George could be so *crabby* sometimes," Sam remarked.

He kept glancing out the window. Then down at the couch. Then at the fireplace. Then at his sneakers. "What are you doing?" I asked.

"I'm memorizing things."

"Oh, yeah, why is that?"

"I'm memorizing this day. So I don't ever forget it." It was 3:45 in the afternoon, Sam added. His sister had left her roller skates by the stairwell. His mother was upstairs, tidying her office. "You're sitting right there," Sam concluded, "and I'm sitting right here."

"Just like I remember where I was when John died," I said.

Sam frowned. "It's not that I'm *going* to forget this day, I just wanted to make really sure."

We sat there for a while longer, the TV droning. "I don't know if this'll make you feel any better," I remarked at one point, "but George was as ready to die as anybody could ever be. I think he actually looked forward to it. He once said, 'We're all just molecules and water, here for a visit.'"

George Harrison lost his valiant struggle with cancer, one reporter was saying.

"Oh, and Sam?" He looked up. "Just so you know, George didn't 'lose' his 'valiant struggle' with cancer. Or his 'courageous fight.' That's just media nonsense. They try to turn everybody who's sick into a winner or a loser. George died of cancer. Period."

A photograph of teenaged George, bone-thin and feral-looking, flicked onscreen. Followed by a clip of George performing with Bob Dylan at the Concert for Bangla Desh. Then George onstage with the Traveling Wilburys, the band he formed in the late 1980s with Bob Dylan, Tom Petty, Jeff Lynne, and Roy Orbison. Now, George was talking to a BBC reporter about his film-production company, Handmade Films. Finally, there he was in a gardener's hat, glancing up from a flower bed. We watched interviews with other musicians — Bono, Paul Simon, and Paul McCartney, who, obviously mindful of his ill-considered remark after John's death, remarked emotionally that George was like "a little brother" to him. Other family friends went on record as saying that in spite of his reputation as "the quiet Beatle," George was anything but. That he was witty. Generous. Private. A family man, who adored his wife, Olivia, and son, Dhani. A lover of ukuleles and Bulgarian choirs.

"I'm going outside to play basketball," Sam said, and he left the room.

Numbed by the story myself, I switched off the TV. For a while, I puttered around the house. I was in search of something. I washed a dish, put in a load of laundry, made a phone call, checked my e-mails, brushed my teeth, put on George's gorgeous acoustic version of "While My Guitar Gently Weeps" from *Anthology 3*. But always that dim tug. I needed to be with someone.

It was strange where the Beatles had taken Sam and me:

sports, for one thing. These days, he and I played tennis, basketball, street hockey. Sports wasn't the draw, though, and neither was competition. It was another excuse to do things together. I joined him outside in the driveway. It was a milky afternoon, English, warm and cold at the same time. A chain saw sounded from down the block; a car rushed past our house, trailed by a middle-aged couple on bikes. It appeared that no one knew that George Harrison had just died. Or maybe they knew and were going about their business anyway. Just as I was doing by playing basketball.

Ten minutes later, Sam and I were halfway through a game of twenty-one, the rules tilted slightly in his favor: because I was a foot and a half taller than he was, I wasn't permitted to block his shots, but I let him block mine. He could travel, stand under the basket for as long as he wanted, and even push me out of the way. Now, he lowered his head and pretended to butt my stomach. "So how are you feeling about all this?" I asked as he clutched me. "About George and all."

"Good." Sam paused. "I mean bad. Sad." Holding the basketball I'd underhanded him, he gazed levelly at me. "It *is* very sad, isn't it?"

"Yeah, it is."

Sam started dribbling, one eye trained on me, the other someplace else. When I thought he was on the verge of charging the basket, a thought would intervene, and he'd grip the ball with both hands. Finally, he came out with it. "I mean, I'm just glad George isn't suffering anymore. Cancer *hurts.* Mom told me that. So I'm just glad he's not in any pain anymore."

"I'm glad about that, too."

He bounced the ball several times, hard. Attempting to dip it under one leg, he lost control, and the ball limped off toward the bushes. Scurrying after it, breathing shallowly, he faced me again, eyes lowered. Making a delicate lunge to my left, dribbling from his left hand back to his right, he wiggled past me, and I let him. He heaved the ball up, missed, shot again, and made it this time. "It's your ball," he said, flipping it back at me.

"He had such a great life, too, Dad. What was he going to do next?" Sam seemed to be asking himself. "What could a person like George Harrison do next? Put out another record? Go on tour again? I mean, he'd already *done* everything in his life."

"I think that's why he turned into a gardener," I said gently. "He said once, 'I'm not really a career person. I'm a gardener, really.' It's strange, isn't it," I went on, "that after becoming what he did, and having the world adore him, that George ended up in his garden. That over the past fifteen, twenty years of his life, the most important thing in the world for him was watching his flowers grow. That should tell you something, shouldn't it?"

"What? What's it supposed to tell you?"

My wisdom hit a snag. "I have no idea," I said politely. "You weren't supposed to ask me that."

• • •

Two of Us

That night, we held an unofficial George-fest: *All Things Must Pass* during dinner, and parts of *The Concert for Bangla Desh* for dessert. I'd never listened to *All Things Must Pass* when it came out, but over the past few months, thanks to Sam, I'd found myself re-appreciating George's solo career. His voice had come a long ways since the days when the other Beatles derided him for his strident Liverpudlian inflections. I thought back to what Sam said once, how ultimately, George's voice was a perfect midpoint between John's and Paul's voices.

Ultimately, though, George Harrison's solo music was too choppy to sustain a celebratory mood. We needed something more cheerful, and so after dinner, Maggie put on "Can't Buy Me Love."

"C'mon," I said, and grabbed Sam's hand. "Let's dance."

Not unexpectedly, my son was loyal to his first instincts. They said *no.* Then, *haven't we been through this?* His arms sagged; his knees slumped. A year and a half had passed since the night he first refused his mother's invitation to partner up, but he was still a boy who preferred playing crazy eights, poker, war, and twenty-one to dancing. Someone who felt more secure outside the fray.

Still, a small struggle seemed to be taking place in his head and his limbs. I have to think that all this death talk had affected him. Somewhere, he must have been mindful of John's death at forty. George's death at sixty. Linda's death at fifty-six. Stuart Sutcliffe's at twenty-two. Not to mention Paul's mother. And John's mother, Julia. And maybe my father, too. The point is, you could never be altogether sure when your life was half over.

The three girls were already out on the floor, dancing in between the stove and the refrigerator. "Can't Buy Me Love" jolted out of the CD player. Paul's song, not George's, but never mind. It was infectious and, finally, irresistible. With a letting-go of something resembling passion, and a refusal to bend down into darkness, Sam put his arms out, tucked in his elbows, and began dancing.

6.
Abbey Road

IT WAS A RADIO SHOW that fired up an idea cooking inside my head.

I was taking a shower one morning and half listening to Elvis Costello and Burt Bacharach reminiscing about their recent musical collaboration. I could barely understand a word of what they were saying: Meter. String overlays. Chord progressions. Harmonics. Minor seconds.

Yet the interview stayed with me over the next few days. I couldn't shake it. I even found a copy on the Internet and forced Maggie to listen to parts. Listening to it reminded me that despite Sam's and my seeming familiarity with the Beatles, we knew practically nothing at all. It wasn't just, as each Beatle was prone to say, that only the four of them knew what *really* happened. It was more that I'd been guilty of the most innocent kind of superficiality.

The Beatles were *musicians*. Not just good-natured, fairytale personalities. Their life, their work, their passion, the reason they wanted fame, had to do with *music:* Chords. Melodies. Bridges. Middle eights.

And wasn't music just the visible tip of what Sam and I knew nothing about? We were up-to-date with a legend. We knew things about the group a lot of people (OK, most people) didn't. We knew some famous stories, some indisputable facts, some probable events. We could match up faces with names and even birthdays, but in the end, we were still relying on our information secondhand. An obsession with the Beatles, or with anything, is an obsession with an *idea.* We'd taken that idea, played with it, mulled it over exhaustively — but gone no further.

Sam could be immoderate in his passions, yet there was a natural point where he braked and turned back. Beatlefest demonstrated that despite his love for the Beatles, his devotion to the band had its limits. Thus my idea — to go to London and Liverpool — felt like a safe bet. It mixed passion *and* perspective, plus it furthered both our interests. We could chisel away the remaining walls that stood between us and the group. We could visit Liverpool, stand outside the Beatles' childhood houses, gawk at their primary schools, catch a whiff of the trains that took them away from their hometown forever. Why not put aside other people's pages and track down the band with our own eyes and ears?

I found Sam upstairs, sprawled on his bedroom rug, surrounded by a battalion of toy soldiers. Elton John's "Good-bye Yellow Brick Road" came out of the speakers. Before I could say a word, Sam's face lit up. "Dad, I was just coming to look for you . . ."

"Well, hey, I must have read your mind."

"What does it mean when Elton John says a person should live their life like a *camel in the wind*?"

"Oh. Actually, I think it's '*candle* in the wind.'"

"Oh." Sam digested this. "No wonder. I mean, what's so great about living your life like a camel in the wind?"

"There's no good reason," I agreed, "to live your life like a camel in the wind." I got to the point. "Sam . . ."

"Uh-huh? Dad, guess how many toy soldiers I have."

"Tons."

"Two hundred seventy-one. I've counted them twice."

"Sam . . . summer vacation."

"What about summer vacation?"

I explained that over July Maggie planned to take Sam's sisters to visit her mother outside Paris. "I was thinking that rather than staying here, maybe you and I could do something around the same time."

"Like what?"

"Like travel somewhere. We could—I don't know—fly to England, hire a tour guide to take us around Liverpool. We could see where the Beatles were born and lived as kids, and all that. See the real Strawberry Field. The real Penny Lane."

When I Googled "Beatles tours" earlier that afternoon, several pages came up. For $2,000 per person, Sam and I could take an eleven-day excursion to "The Beatles' Eng-

land," which included a night at the Casbah Coffee Shop in
Liverpool with Pete Best as our host, and a drunken ramble
along the "Beatle Ale Trail." Another jaunt offered guests
their own John-and-Yoko-inspired "bed-in" at the Amsterdam Hilton, along with a canal trip, a "Twist 'n' Shout
Dance Party" at the Hard Rock Café in London, and a "personal meet and greet with Pete Best" (if nothing else, I now
knew what Pete Best was up to these days). There was a
Beatles-themed cruise to the Sea of Cortez in Mexico, even
a Liverpool-based "fab, gear, groovy, cool, out-of-sight corporate teambuilding workshop" touching upon "personality
conflicts within a team," "achieving more creative solutions
to work-based problems," and "low commitment and team
morale."

But I didn't like groups or crowds or corporate buzz-
words, and many of these tours sounded kind of boozy, too.
I thought it might be more fun to improvise. "So what do
you think about you and me traveling together?"

"Just us?"

"Uh-huh."

His forehead furrowed. "So the girls wouldn't come at
all?" Sam had recently taken up my habit of calling his
mother and sisters *the girls.*

"Yup, that's right."

"I'd love it."

"Mom—I mean, Dad—d'you know what I really, really
love?"

It was midsummer, and Maggie was in France with Sam's sisters. "What?" I said.

My son and I were sitting in a hip, albeit deserted, Italian restaurant in Notting Hill, eating design-your-own pizzas and drinking sodas.

"Jet lag," Sam went on. "I like the feeling of the sheets when you're really, really tired." He leaned across the table and made a confession. "You know, I turn my pillow over during the night sometimes because I'm looking for a cold spot to put my ear on?"

"I do that, too. I *love* the cold spot."

"Dad, you and I are so alike it's not even *funny.*"

We'd pulled up in front of our Holland Park hotel early that morning, checked into our second-floor minisuite, and fallen almost immediately asleep on side-by-side twin beds. London was chilly and overcast and crowded. When I woke up, disoriented and hungry, it was nearly four in the afternoon, and the sun shone weakly through lightly breathing shades.

Despite our nearly seven-hour nap, Sam looked exhausted, as if he'd parachuted into England. I'd forgotten to pack him a belt, and when his cargo pants kept threatening to shimmy down his hips, I offered him one of my neckties. With his matted, uncombed hair, and the tie's red-striped short end drooping down one side, he looked appropriately hippified, the scion of a bearded carpenter and his master-weaver-wife.

Probably as a result of his fatigue, non sequiturs flowed from him. Between bites of his pizza, he asked me to explain the difference between anchovies and sardines. Also, how many gallons of milk a day did a single cow produce? How much was Oprah Winfrey worth, and why had her parents decided to name her that? I wasn't sure of the answer to any of these questions, but that didn't stop him from asking more. What was the most disgusting thing I'd ever eaten? What part of pigs was inside hot dogs? Who invented futons?

This kind of interrogation wasn't at all unusual for him, but I was surprised that it contained no Beatles-related queries. Despite his initial thumbs-up, Sam had become surprisingly ambivalent about coming to London and Liverpool. Whenever the subject came up, he offered a small smile and a cautious, "It'll be fun." I attributed this seeming neutrality to his love of being at home and to the long, good year he'd had at a new school. He was enjoying hanging around our house doing summery things—playing basketball and Gameboy; riding his bike and scooter; hanging out with his best friend, Alex; or just lazing in the hammock with a book.

Several times, I'd had to remind him that we'd be in England during the last week of July and that he shouldn't schedule any play dates or sleepovers during that time. But he kept forgetting.

"Sam, do you not *want* to go?" I asked him point-blank one night.

"Do *you*?" he parried softly. When I nodded, Sam wrinkled his forehead. "I'm just not sure what we're going to *do* when we *get* there, that's all."

I explained that we were going to visit the new British Library to see the permanent exhibit of Beatles lyrics. I'd also arranged for us to go on a pair of Beatles walks, two-hour-long rambles on streets and past buildings that had played a big part in the group's life. The founder of the London Beatles Fan Club, one Richard Porter, led them both. Afterward, we'd hop aboard a train to Liverpool, spend a couple of days there, return to London, then fly home.

"Oh, OK." He seemed to have been expecting something more traumatic.

Sam, it was becoming clear, had reached an inevitable Beatles plateau. It happened. You couldn't avoid it. Hearing familiar songs over and over again didn't satisfy the human desire for novelty, or for exploring other music. In an attempt to invigorate our Beatles collection, I tried to order some new bootlegs, but Billy Shears's old Web site yielded the message, "Check the URL and try again." Browsing in a used-record store, I found a three-CD set titled *Beatles Rarities,* but much of it comprised fumbling conversation, distant chuckles, and the muffled voices of engineers and sound men. Next, I'd brought home some of the oddball musical projects the band had inspired over the years. Beatles Gregorian chant. Caribbean steel drum Beatles. Beatles songs played by dulcimers and flutes. *Beatles a La Latin. Alvin and the Chipmunks Sing the Beatles.* Most of these things ended up unplayed in the CD holder, but at least I felt I was keeping a certain momentum going.

Overnight, it seemed, Sam had started to focus more on boy stuff—an antique bayonet his step-grandfather had showed him how to use during a visit to Texas, his twice-a-week fencing classes, tennis lessons, and reading about the tanks and aircraft of World War II. For his ninth birthday, he'd requested no music, just books, toy soldiers, a bow and arrow, and a set of walkie-talkies. He was either planning a siege of some kind or his interests were changing.

"You're growing up so fast," I'd remark to him. Sam seemed pleased by this; compared to school, he found the world of adults sunlit and easy. I could tell the sentiment in my voice confused him, so I took pains to explain. It wasn't that he *shouldn't* grow up. I was happy another year had passed and he was still the same wonderful, kind-hearted person. But I was sad about the little boy vanishing under the long arms and legs that filled the couch at night. "When you're a dad someday, you'll know what I mean," I said.

And did it really matter if Sam was taking a vacation from the Beatles? There was no way anyone could keep up that kind of obsessive preoccupation. But I worried that without them Sam and I would begin groping for common ground again, that, basically, if my son broke up with the Beatles, he'd break up with me, too.

The waiter came. "Dad," Sam blurted out as I was ordering coffee. "Could I have a cup, too?"

He'd never expressed any interest in coffee before. In fact, hadn't he once vowed never to drink the stuff? "Well, of course," I said at last. "It just . . . keeps you up. It's sort of an adult thing. And caffeine is kind of addicting. It's a *nice* addiction, as far as addictions go, it's just—"

"Can I or can't I?"

Again, a slight pang in my chest at how grown-up he was getting. "Two coffees, please," I said to the waiter.

When it arrived, Sam stared down at the cup. "So . . . what do I do now?"

"You can add milk. Or sugar. Actually, in this case, both might be a good idea."

"But *you* don't drink it with either of those things."

When I told him I took it black, he said stubbornly, "Then *I* want to try it that way, too."

He took a sip, then shuddered. "Actually, I *will* try it with milk and sugar."

Later in the hotel room, I took a long shower, and twenty minutes later, emerged dripping into the room. "Hi," Sam called over happily. He was busy setting up the platoon of green plastic soldiers he'd brought from home. A dozen snipers knelt along the radiator. Two dozen more rested atop the television set, with several other battalions scattered among the cups, saucers, and plug-in kettle on the dresser.

"How many soldiers are in this room with us?" I asked.

Sam smiled mysteriously. "Enough." Then, "Dad . . ."

"Uh-huh?"

"If you get up really early in the morning, can you wake me up, too?"

"You don't want to sleep in?" I asked. "You're on vacation here, remember?"

No; he wanted to get up when I did; that way, we could have our morning cup of coffee together. "I like coffee," he added. "It makes me think more quickly. Plus, coffee can be my warmer." He shivered. "It's cold in England."

The British Library's Treasures Collection was tranquil and decorously lit. It was a phenomenal collection of stuff, from early folios of Shakespeare plays to original manuscripts by the Brontës to a mound of dark wood revealed to be Jane Austen's writing desk. Here was the Gutenberg Bible. The Magna Carta. Lewis Carroll's original *Through the Looking Glass.* Not to mention wilted manuscripts by Wilfred Owen, Laurence Sterne, and Goethe, even one of James Joyce's notebooks, containing a crossed-out page from *Finnegans Wake.*

That was just the literature exhibit. The music gallery boasted sheet music of Chopin and from Handel's *Messiah,* as well as Beethoven's sketches for the *Pastoral* Symphony. Sam was engrossed in the Beethoven folio—unlike me, he could read music—when I happened upon what he and I had come to see.

The lyrics were scratched, scrawled, inked, and penciled on napkins, memo pads, and scrap paper. There were fragments of four lines, six lines, eight lines, and in a couple of cases, the entire song. Some had working titles, fiercely underlined; others didn't. Without melodies attached, the words seemed slight, occasionally silly, and mesmerizingly familiar: "*Michelle / these are words that . . .*" "*Day after day / alone on a hill . . .*" "*There are places I remember . . .*" "*She's got a ticket to ride . . .*" "*My baby don't care . . .*"

"Jesus," I called over to Sam without thinking. "Look at this."

I don't know how long I stared down at the words. I was hypnotized. Captured in bedrooms, living rooms, kitchens, sound studios, and coffee shops, many of the words looked green and juvenile. For a brief, insane moment, they made me think, *Hey, I could do that!* Then I realized: here was where most guys under the age of fifty first learned about women, and what they could do to you, whether it was holding your hand or really getting a hold on you or putting you down or loving you (do); the list was endless.

Sam had joined me. "These are the *original lyrics,*" I kept saying. "This is, like, *flabbergasting* to me."

I moved on, but kept circling back to the Beatles exhibit. I couldn't help but think how happy John Lennon would be to find that his words sat only twenty feet away from Lewis Carroll's, one of his early literary heroes. Carroll's "The Walrus and the Carpenter," in fact, had inspired Lennon's "I Am the Walrus." Nobody here today appeared as impressed by Carroll's work; *Through the Looking Glass* was deserted. Most visitors bypassed the Magna Carta. They skipped past the selection from Leonardo's notebooks, the Sherborne Missal (c. 1400), the Barcelona Haggadah (c. 1350), and the Lindisfarne Gospels (c. 950). Of the dozen or so people in the room, three-quarters of us were trained on the Beatles exhibit. We instinctively gave one another breathing room. No crowding, no shoving. If you saw someone praying in a church, you didn't slide into the pew and say "Shove over," did you?

Sam scanned the Beatles lyrics. "Wow," he said. "That's neat." Then, "Dad, come see the Chopin."

"Just one second." Please—I just wanted to stare at the lyrics a little longer.

"Dad . . ." Sam was tugging at me now, his grip surprisingly strong. "Fred-er-ic *Chopin.*"

The high-ceilinged, recently refurbished Marlyebone tube station resembles a chic, airy underground shopping mall more than it does a commuter train and subway terminal. Inside are several upscale places to snack, plenty of clean benches, a florist, and a small Fortnum & Mason store. Sam and I were sunning ourselves outside on a ledge when I caught sight of our Beatles walking-tour guide trundling through the entryway, a black waist pouch bound tightly to one of his belt loops. I knew immediately it was him, since he'd uploaded a photograph of himself posing with Paul McCartney onto his Web site. "That's our guy, Richard Porter," I whispered to Sam.

He whispered back, "I'm going to go spy on him," and he ducked inside Marlyebone Station. He returned a couple of minutes later with a report. "He's just standing there by the flower shop."

"OK, let's move out," I whispered.

Just as Sam had reported, Richard stood a few yards away from a florist. Grimacing stiffly, he held up a sheaf of leaflets. When I introduced myself, Richard nodded coolly, his grimace frozen in place.

A few more people joined us—couples mostly, as well as a young mother holding a huge, pink baby. In the end, about a dozen of us were gathered awkwardly around Richard, who kept his leaflets raised high, like a trophy he'd spent a lifetime pursuing. He was a compact, puckish, thirty-something man with the brown, pouffy hair and faintly pocked skin of a 1950s adolescent. He seemed to have a contentious inner life. His mouth twitched in subtle, perennial motion. His eyes would narrow, then widen again, as if in surprise. It was as though he were rehearsing a series of prickly conversations with imaginary authorities or enemies.

Richard introduced himself to our group: he was the founder of the London Beatles Fan Club, the current holder of the title "Beatles Brain of Britain," and the author of *The Abbey Road Café Guide to the Beatles' London,* which he would be happy to autograph at the end of the tour.

He led us just outside the station and stopped in front of a drab alley. This, he announced, was Boston Street, a site that, along with Marlyebone Station, was used as a backdrop for scenes from *A Hard Day's Night.* Flopping open his binder, Richard showed a few stills from the movie and added that the old-fashioned phone booth glimpsed in the opening scenes was later torn down to make room for the little Fortnum & Mason.

Sam must have sat through *A Hard Day's Night* at least half a dozen times, though not recently. "Do you remember this place?" I asked him. "Remember the Beatles running for their lives with all those fans chasing them?"

He pursed his forehead. "Sort of," he said. "*A Hard Day's Night.* No, wait, I'm thinking of *Help!*" Sam mock-banged himself on his forehead. "Right, *A Hard Day's Night.* Sorry."

Sam wasn't very excited by this glimpse of Beatles history, but that was OK, I guessed. It was just an alleyway. We were off again.

Richard strode purposefully ahead, glancing neither left nor right, with the rest of us straggling behind, and Sam bringing up the rear. He caught up with us just as Richard halted in front of the Westminster Registry Office, formerly known as the Marylebone Register. Here, in March of 1969, Paul McCartney married the former Linda Eastman while several hundred female fans amassed outside, weeping hysterically. Five months after John Lennon died, Richard went on, Ringo Starr married his second wife, the actress Barbara Bach, here. As Richard opened up his binder to show us photographs from the two weddings, an old, unshaven man on a bench behind us chuckled mirthlessly and raised a half-empty bottle of Dewar's. A few members of our entourage sidled away from him.

"The question I'm asked most often is whether or not I've ever met a Beatle," Richard declaimed. He had an auctioneer's brash, emphatic voice. Triumphantly, he opened his binder again. "So here's a nice picture of me with Paul!"

We crowded in to ogle Richard's photograph. The picture was a duplicate of the one I'd seen on his Web site. It showed Paul, wearing a seersucker jacket over a black T-shirt, posed beside a younger, much happier-looking Richard. There was more where that came from, including a photograph of Linda McCartney gazing warily at the camera. "But don't think there's a possibility of any of *you* meeting a Beatle today," Richard crowed. "Ringo lives in the south of France, and Paul is in the U.S. right now!"

Time to move along. This was kind of fun, I thought, and dropped back to keep pace with Sam. He's a meditative walker at the best of times, as though he forgets occasionally where he's going or gets distracted mid-step. "Are you OK?" I asked. "Do you want to stop and take a little rest or something?"

"I'm just a little tired, that's all."

"Don't you find all this kind of fascinating?"

"Dad . . ." Sam's voice was suddenly urgent.

"Uh-huh?"

"What temperature is the average freezer at? Is it zero degrees, or minus zero degrees, or minus two hundred degrees?"

Swallowing my surprise, I said, "Um, I'm not really sure."

"Can you guess?"

"Extremely cold," I said lamely. "At least thirty-two degrees, which is the temperature water freezes at. I don't know the precise number, though."

This conversation blocked out most of Richard's lecture on the former site of the Apple Boutique at 94 Baker Street, which the Beatles bought for tax reasons (the band was then being taxed at 95 percent of its income). Designed, in Paul's words, as "a beautiful place where you could buy beautiful things," the store sold designer clothing and hippie accessories, but hemorrhaged so much money it closed eight months later. I regained my equilibrium only when we entered the quiet upscale neighborhood of Montagu Square. We stopped at a building marked number 34. Here, Richard asked us to train our eyes on the basement and first-floor apartments. Ringo Starr moved to this address in 1965 with his first wife, Maureen, and though Ringo would eventually relocate to suburban Weybridge, he maintained this apartment as a crash pad for himself and assorted friends, including Jimi Hendrix. This was also where Paul composed "Eleanor Rigby," and where John and Yoko posed naked for the cover of their album *Unfinished Music Volume One: Two Virgins.*

The chairman of EMI, Sir Joseph Lockwood, was extremely distressed about the *Two Virgins* cover, Richard went on, reportedly saying to John, "If you were doing this for art, you could at least put some better-looking bodies on the cover. Why not get Paul to do it? Or use statues from the park?"

Sam had never seen the *Two Virgins* album close-up, though certainly he'd read about it (there were a few Beatles artifacts I censored from him).

"Paul wrote 'Eleanor Rigby' in there," I repeated to Sam, pointing at the basement window.

"Cool," Sam said. "I like 'Eleanor Rigby.'" It was time to move along again.

High above my head, from the top windows of a building opposite number 57 Wimpole Street—the former family home of actress Jane Asher—a madman began hollering at our little group. His voice was incoherent, but its message was clear: *I'm sick of you people in my neighborhood.* Still, Richard's loud voice easily drowned him out. Paul lived here with the Asher family for three years in the mid 1960s, Richard explained, and wrote many songs here, including

"Yesterday" and "I Want to Hold Your Hand." Paul often dodged love-struck female fans by tiptoeing from his bedroom window along a ledge, ducking into a neighbor's apartment, and making his way down to the sidewalk, where he'd climb into a waiting car.

Trying to get a laugh, I whispered to Sam, *"Scrambled eggs. Oh baby how I love your legs . . ."* He just smiled diffidently and glanced down.

"Do you remember reading about Jane Asher?" I went on. "She was an actress? She went out with Paul for a long time in the sixties? Her brother Peter Asher was in a group called 'Peter and Gordon,' and then he became James Taylor's manager?"

Sam nodded somberly. "Oh, that's right."

He was about to say something else when I noticed that Richard was calling for quiet. It was time, he announced dramatically, to board the tube. We would take the Jubilee Line one stop, to St. John's Wood Station, and from there walk to Abbey Road Studios.

As Richard Porter strode out of the St. John's Wood tube station, with our group traipsing behind him like day-care children, I couldn't help wondering how many times he'd made this same excursion along this same sidewalk. A thousand? Two thousand? Trundling along a curving residential street, with the rest of us in ardent, if confused, pursuit, he came to a stop at a three-way intersection. "Where do you think we are?" I whispered to Sam.

After the bustle of Baker Street, this lethargic triangle of northwestern London felt dozing, refined. With their bow windows and haughty porticos, the Regency and Victorian houses were separated from the street by high fences, camouflaging bushes, and meandering walkways. I was not surprised to discover in one of my guidebooks that London courtesans once found St. John's Wood's quiet and discretion conducive to their work.

Richard's braying voice suddenly drew my attention. We were here. This was it. Welcome, that is, to Abbey Road.

For the first time that morning, Sam seemed to come alive. He squinted first in puzzlement, then delight, and a slow smile spread across his face. "Wait . . ." he whispered, "you mean this is the actual place on the record cover?"

"Yes!"

"But I didn't know you could *come* here! I thought it would be a *monument* or something. Why didn't you tell me?"

"I *did* tell you!" And I had, three or four times.

The entire group's lethargy seemed to have lifted. We'd taken a two-minute subway ride and entered a forty-year-old record cover. Once I'd known every fleck and crack in its worn pavement, the summery bulge of its trees, its pure blue sky. On the crosswalk, George looked like an unpretentious farmer; Paul a hip, jaded bridegroom; Ringo a college valedictorian; John spectrally white, lanky and strange. On the back, the cover said, simply, *Beatles,* followed by *Abbey Rd. N.* The rest was obscured by the ghostly blur of a passerby's coat, a Paul-is-dead clue if there ever was one.

Most of the men in our group appeared suddenly at a

loss. They beamed or looked embarrassed or looked to their female companions for help in containing, or naming, what was going on in their heads. Others simply stared at the crosswalk stripes in fond disbelief. A few couples embraced, and behind me, two twenty-something couples kissed with the intensity of a couple reunited after a world war.

I wished Maggie were here with me.

"I can't believe this place actually exists," Sam kept saying. I kept saying, "I know, isn't this great?"

Holding up one hand against the oncoming cars, Richard marched confidently across the zebra stripes, with the rest of us following shyly behind. Before crossing, Sam lingered a little on the sidewalk; this was OK?, his eyes asked. "C'mon," I said, "hold onto me," and we crossed together.

"Be extremely careful about cars," Richard warned us more than once, adding that when the Beatles posed for the *Abbey Road* sleeve in the summer of 1969, a cop was on hand to keep the traffic from hitting the photographer, who was perched atop a stepladder in the middle of the road. Several fans, in fact, had been killed trying to re-create the crossing scene.

While the rest of us crossed, one man stayed behind on the sidewalk and took off his socks and shoes. Daintily raising his pants' cuffs, and waiting a moment for traffic to subside, he gingerly tiptoed across the crosswalk, then retreated back to where his shoes, socks, and female friend were waiting. "Had to be done!" he called out cheerfully.

Now we were all clustered in front of a graffiti-laden,

white stone wall, behind which stood the black-gated Abbey Road–EMI Studios. Richard explained that *Abbey Road*'s original working title was "Everest," a reference not to the mountain, but to the brand of cigarettes that Beatles engineer Geoff Emerick smoked. Unfortunately, Studio 2, where the Beatles recorded most of their songs, wasn't visible from the street. But we could see Studio 1, where in 1967, the Beatles broadcast "All You Need Is Love" to a global audience of approximately four hundred million people, and where they spent nearly eight hours recording "A Day in the Life" with the assistance of a full orchestra.

The fence, which is scrubbed every few months to make room for new graffiti, served as a makeshift Beatles shrine. Messages ranged from the obvious—*I wanna hold your hand, Paul* and *One sweet dream came true today*—to the fancifully topical—*Rock on from the Potters! Love, Harry et al.*—to the unnerving—*Help me* and *Right on, Charlie Manson!* and *I'll join you soon, George.*

Sam scurried up next to me. "Dad . . ."

"Yuh-huh?"

"When I was crossing the street, I kept wondering, Am I stepping exactly where one of the Beatles stepped?"

"I'll bet you were," I said. "Whose footprint do you think your sneaker was touching?"

He smiled shyly. "George's."

Briefly, he knelt to scan the messages on the wall, then straightened up. "Dad, d'you have something to write with?"

When I handed him a pen, Sam wrote, "SLS and PJS,"

followed by the date. "There!" he said with delight, handing me back the pen.

"Thanks, Sam," I said.

The Beatles walk was officially over. The members of our group trickled off in all directions, and Richard Porter strode off toward the St. John's Wood train station. Sam and I were the only ones left.

"You know, Paul McCartney lives in this neighborhood," I said. "Pretty close to here, actually." I reminded Sam that Paul was the only Beatle barefoot on the *Abbey Road* cover. "Paul always said it wasn't because he was dead—"

"Dad, I know that—"

"—but because it was a beautiful summer's day, and he'd taken his shoes off just for the heck of it." I paused. "So . . . do you want to see Paul's house?"

"Do you?"

"It's your call."

Sam shook his head. "Dad, if you were Paul McCartney, would you like people standing outside your house—"

"Not really—"

"—and taking pictures of your front door and your windows and your lawn?"

"I would hate that. You're right. We'll leave him alone."

"Mom—I mean, Dad," Sam said later that afternoon. "Are you absolutely *positive* it's OK for me to go?"

"Sure. It's the only chance you'll have to see him. Plus, you guys always get along so great."

For the past few weeks, and especially since we'd arrived in London, Sam had been addressing me confusedly as "Mom," before correcting himself. At first, I was almost shocked. What did this mean? Was he missing Maggie that much? Fathers, I knew, were custodians of some mythical big picture. "How was school today?" I'd ask the kids. The replies would generally be the same: "Fine." "Terrible." "So-so." But when Maggie asked them the same question, their replies were detailed, excruciatingly exact — the way, in fact, Sam had been addressing me recently. I took it as the ultimate compliment. He could call me "Mom" all he wanted.

Though I admit: I was taken aback when he asked Mom —"Sorry, I mean, *Dad*"—if he could skip the second Beatles walk in favor of a play date with the son of London friends. They were planning a daytrip to the Imperial War Museum and had left a message at the front desk inviting him.

"Could we call Mom?" Sam asked now.

"You mean Dad?" I couldn't help but ask. Sam made a face at me as he dialed. He and Maggie and his two sisters spoke for a long time, Sam's voice enthusiastic; then he cupped the receiver. "Mom wants to know how we're doing."

"Tell her we're doing terribly," I called over.

"Dad says to tell you we're doing terribly. Yeah, me, especially. I hate London. Dad's a nightmare." Sam proceeded to describe the Beatles walk in detail (he'd been paying more attention than I thought), then told her about his upcoming visit to the Imperial War Museum. Now it was my turn to assure Maggie that we were fine.

We were doing better than fine, actually, but Maggie mightn't have thought so if she'd seen us at that moment. This was the first time Sam and I had traveled alone together. Almost automatically, we became raffish coconspirators, our beds summer-camp bunks, our room a combination frat house, Laundromat, pre-recycling center, and multimedia room. We slept late, spoke to one another in subhuman Cockney accents, and bought greasy snacks and blood orange juice from the supermarket across the street. We reveled in our shared love of slacking off at a nearby video game parlor. If Maggie were here, Sam's clothes would be folded neatly in a dresser drawer. His toothbrush and toothpaste would be waiting for him inside a glass by the sink. But under my watch, his clothes were strewn everywhere. A few had landed in the gap between our beds. Nearly two hundred plastic green snipers scowled at us from every available surface. And my side, consisting of empty water bottles, crumpled chip bags, and screaming English tabloids, wasn't much better. Sam was right: except for how we took our coffee, he and I were quite similar.

The only difference was that I was eager to go on the second Beatles walk, and Sam wasn't.

Richard Porter seemed overnight to have become one of the most sought-after men in London.

If ever a walk could be termed "standing room only," today's was it. Hoisting myself up on the plastic lid of an overflowing garbage can beside the Tottenham Court tube station the next morning, I gazed on in quiet disbelief as

men, women, teenagers, college kids, and entire families en-
gulfed the island just underneath the marquee of the Do-
minion Theatre. Yesterday, there were barely a dozen of us;
today I counted fifty-two.

Once Richard had gotten through his introductory spiel,
we set off toward the London Palladium. For the first half-
hour or so, I savored my newfound independence, and I
imagined Sam was doing the same. I could walk along at
my own pace. I could gaze into shop windows. I could
strike up conversations with other walkers if I felt like it.
Plus, I doubted Sam would have gotten too excited by the
Palladium, site of the 1963 TV appearance that incited the
fanaticism called "Beatlemania."

As Richard was shooing us along to the next location—
"C'mon, remember you're not the only people on the sidewalk"—I noticed a couple of other walkers, an attractive,
short-haired woman in her mid thirties accompanied a
young boy, presumably her son. He had a buzz cut and
looked to be around Sam's age. As I looked on, he scooted
underneath the Palladium's marquee, removed his dark
glasses, and gazed out animatedly at his mother's camera.
"Move a little bit to the left, Jacob," she called out. She was
either American or Canadian. "And remember, it wouldn't
kill you to smile."

Jacob obliged. When she'd gotten her picture, he tipped
his dark glasses back onto his nose and rejoined her on the
far sidewalk.

Suddenly I missed Sam deeply. My nostalgia intensified
as we trooped through tranquil Soho Square and arrived at

the smaller-than-expected headquarters of MPL Communications. This, one of the largest privately owned, independent music publishing companies in the world, was the epicenter of Paul's songwriting empire, Richard told us, which today includes proprietorship of nearly twenty-five thousand songs, including the scores to *Annie, A Chorus Line, Grease,* and *Guys and Dolls* (not to mention such tunes as "Hike! Notre Dame," "Once in Love with Amy," and "Walking in the Park with Eloise"). My fellow walkers lunged forward as Richard again produced the photographs of himself posing with Paul. Jacob, I saw, was right up front. "When Paul saw this photo of us, he said, 'Weren't we a lovely couple?' Typical McCartney humor," Richard added with atypical shyness.

Jacob posed for a second photograph in front of MPL, then jogged up ahead to walk side by side with Richard. Meanwhile, I fell into step with Jacob's mother. "So your son must be a huge Beatles fan?" I said.

"Oh, the biggest," she said. Her smile was proud, a little helpless. Her son had been a full-fledged Beatles nut since the age of seven, when his father first played *Sgt. Pepper* in the living room. "He just . . ." she wrestled to find the words, "can't get enough of them."

"So what do you think it is?" I said finally. "Why do you think it's the Beatles? Why not the Who or Led Zeppelin or the Rolling Stones? Why not a hundred other bands?"

"I don't know," she said slowly. "I think it's . . ." She hesitated. "Well, they're *good,* for one thing. And they were nice people, too, weren't they? They weren't monsters." She looked as though she was about to say more, but in the end, she shook her head and let the question expire. "It's one of those mysteries. They were the *Beatles,* right?"

After a visit to the mural at the entrance to Carnaby Street, the Broadwick Street toilets where John Lennon once appeared in a comedy sketch with Peter Cook and Dudley Moore, and the former Trident Studios, now renamed The Sound Studio, where the Beatles recorded "Hey Jude," it was time, once again, for the group to board the Jubilee Line to the St. John's Wood tube station. I was half tempted to go up to Abbey Road again, but decided against it. I wanted to see Sam. When I picked him up from his play date in Shepherd's Bush, he didn't want to go back to the hotel. In fact, his friend wanted him to stay the night; it was fine with his friend's mother if it was OK with me. "Please, Dad?" Sam asked.

"Sorry," I said, "but no. We're going to Liverpool, remember?"

"Oh, that's right," Sam said, clearly disappointed.

On the way through Holland Park, I came right out with it: "So, Sam, do you *not* want to go to Liverpool?"

"No, I do. I'm sorry. I just couldn't remember when we were going, that's all. How was the second Beatles tour?"

"It was good," I said. "I missed you."

"I missed you, too. Though I *did* have fun." He paused. "Thanks for letting me go."

Sam put an object in my left palm. After a second or

two, I realized it was his hand. It made a perfect, unselfconscious fit. It felt as good and comfortable there as a baseball in a mitt. When I glanced down at him, I could think of only one word to describe how he looked: *content.* I felt the same way.

"Do you know what I saw on today's Beatles walk?" I asked. "The building where they played the rooftop concert in *Let It Be.*"

"Really?"

"Yeah. And it was really *small,* too. Why is everything always smaller than you think it's going to be?"

I remembered reading once how George had stormed out of Apple Studios one night because "It just wasn't fun anymore." Ringo had done the same during the recording of *The White Album* because he felt underappreciated. "No one," Ringo remarked later, "ever said to me, 'You're great.'"

"I'm not sure if I've ever told you this," I said to Sam as we passed behind a bus kiosk, "but I think you're a wonderful kid."

Sam smiled and glanced downward. "No, Dad, *you're* a wonderful kid."

"I'm a grownup."

"Well, you *act* like a kid."

"I mean that, though, Sam. I want to make sure you knew that from me. Because I forget, I get busy sometimes, I forget to tell you that kind of stuff. I think it, but I don't say it. I think you're great. And I feel really, really lucky and honored to have you as my son."

It was a speech my father might have given me once, but

didn't. I wasn't going to let another day go by without getting the words out.

"Thanks," Sam said, and he tightened his grip.

We passed by our hotel, but neither Sam nor I remarked on it. And then as we made our way into Notting Hill, I had one of those weird epiphanies. It was simple, obvious: even if you didn't get what you wanted from your own dad, you were under no obligation to carry on the paternal tradition. You could stop it. Right there. Just stick out your foot and trip it. Start all over again.

It wasn't an easy revelation. Or a perfect one. It was muddier, fiercer than that. It felt, in fact, like a little ghost step across my chest, then off again. It pinched, but as my dad's generation might have done, I sucked it up and took a long breath. And then I let that generation go.

So it was never my lot to have the ideal father-son friendship. So it sometimes felt lonely trying to give to someone, your son, the things *you* wanted but only got a little of yourself. So, too bad. Get over it. You wouldn't have known what was right to give your own son if you didn't know the difference. Your father was magnificent in so many ways, but like you, he was comically imperfect. He was gone; I was here. I wasn't "Dad of the Year" yet. There were still a few frozen streaks inside me, outside the sun's reach, but I had warmed up. Now I was doing a good job. Maybe there was no one to tell me that, but I believed it, and it might even have been the truth.

"My father would've really loved you, too," I said to Sam. "I just wish you could have met him and he could have met you." A tear slid down my face.

I'd seen my father cry only once. Sam, I knew, had seen me cry a couple of times — once when I was reading *Romeo and Juliet* aloud to him before bed, another time when I was watching *Father of the Bride* with Steve Martin. My son kept walking as we crossed an intersection, and then his hand, which had dropped away, found mine again.

"Dad, d'you want to stop somewhere and get something to drink? Some coffee? Or a Sprite or something?"

"I'm fine," I said. And I was. "I'm sorry." But there was nothing to apologize for.

I remember reading more than one interview with Paul McCartney in which he brought up a moment from his childhood for which he's never been able to forgive himself. Paul is the first to admit his family was socially upwardly mobile — his parents, Jim and Mary, naturally wanted their two sons to receive a better shake in life than they'd had — and in 1955, the family moved from the Liverpool suburb of Speke to the relatively upscale neighborhood of Allerton. One day, Mary McCartney pronounced the word "ask" in an accent that her young son perceived as "posh." Paul parroted her pronunciation back at her. Mary McCartney blushed and looked away, Paul remembered. A few months later, she was dead of breast cancer. Yes, he was sure she knew he didn't mean anything by his mimicry, but more than fifty years later, Paul never forgave himself, referring to it in one interview as "a terrible little thing," the one thing he kept wishing over the years he could take back.

On a visit to England when I was about fifteen, my father took my mother, my sister, and me to see his old air force base somewhere in Hertfordshire. He rented a small car and we drove through the rolling English countryside. At last we pulled up in front of his old base. Since the war, it had become, improbably, a greyhound racing track. My sister and I laughed hysterically and teased my father for the rest of the trip. But after that, my dad, I realized now, barely ever mentioned his war experiences again.

Paul's mother was dead and my father was too. One day, no one at all would remember a half-century-old imitation, or a nearly thirty-year-old laugh from the back seat of a tiny car. And until that time came, we'd live with it.

I took Sam's shoulders and steered him toward our hotel. "We have to get up early tomorrow, remember?" I said. "Our train leaves at eight."

7.
Let
It Be

AS OUR TRAIN ROLLED through the English countryside early the next morning, Sam busied himself by setting up his army men along the arm of his seat. As the train sped up, the snipers on the ashtray lid made a rapid vibrating sound. We were passing through green farmland now, and the lambs and horses on either side of us didn't bother glancing up to see yet another train rush by.

"Dad, thanks so much for this trip," Sam interjected at one point. He was snacking on a bag of vinegar potato chips he'd picked out from the snack trolley.

"Thank *you* for coming with me. I can't really imagine doing this by myself."

"I like it when it's just you and me," he went on between munches. "No girls. I mean, I like Mom and Lily and Susannah and all, but I like just being with you the most."

"I like being with you, too," I said. "You're a lot of fun to travel with. Because you like to — I don't know — *hang out.* Not feel you have to visit churches and cathedrals and graveyards and stuff like that."

"Right, 'cause we haven't seen all that much tourist stuff, have we?"

"No, but we've had some *excellent* pizza."

Nuneaton. Stafford. Crewe. Runcorn. Next stop Liverpool. Around Runcorn, livid clouds began forming over the hills, like bruises on skin, and then the hills went away and were replaced by a gradual flattening and an increase in dissolute-looking industry. "We're going to the Toppermost of the Poppermost, Lad!" I said to Sam at one point. These were words John used to say early in the Beatles' career, to rev up his bandmates' flagging spirits. "So, what do you think Penny Lane looks like in person?" I asked, and when Sam didn't answer, I added, "I've always pictured this frantic, sweet, cheerful place. Sort of circuslike."

My attempt to get a little Beatles momentum going sounded slightly artificial, but Sam didn't notice. "Dad," he said solemnly, "in your opinion who was the better leader: F.D.R. or Churchill?"

"They were both great leaders. They both kept their countries going during an incredibly difficult time in history."

"More difficult than now?"

"Believe it or not, yes."

"Dad, can we watch *Patton* when we get home?"

It was one of my father's favorite movies. "Absolutely," I said. "We can rent it." There was, it seemed, still no way around the Second World War. We were en route to a port city nearly brought to its knees by the German Luftwaffe, heading back into the source of what I suspected was my father's greatest exhilaration, and the source of his silence.

Sam's thoughts appeared lodged in distant battlefields, and I was happy to meet him halfway. Did he know that between 1940 and 1942, Liverpool was shelled almost nightly, making it the most bombed English city apart from London? That if England hadn't abolished the draft in 1960 there might have been no Beatles, since they would have been called up, preventing them from forming a band?

Twenty minutes outside Lime Street Station, the windows of the train began to speck, then crawl with rain, and then at last, Liverpool appeared out the right-hand window. It appeared an unbroken phantasm of misted roofs and black-burned chimneys. The train slowed down as it entered a long tunnel, and then Sam and I were disembarking along with the two dozen or so remaining passengers into Lime Street Station.

Hillary, a plump, middle-aged Liverpudlian, and a twenty-two-year veteran of the Beatles tourism trade, was there to greet us. "Hullo, Sam," she said warmly as we packed ourselves inside her little car. "Are you ready to see what the Beatles saw when *they* were nine years old?"

He nodded amiably, and gazed out the back window. Though it was midday at the end of July, Liverpool was freezing. There was a toxic smell in the air, which I made the mistake of mentioning to Hillary. "It's probably caused by all this rain," she replied with sudden guardedness. From then on she made it a point to pump up her hometown. "There's *lots* happening here," she boasted. "Five new hotels just in the last year." Liverpool, she went on, was currently a candidate for the country's Capital of Culture Prize (the CEO of the Liverpool Culture Company later emphasized that Liverpool was promoting every cultural amenity it offered "short of getting smashed on a Saturday night").

During the tour's first half, we drove past the modest, terraced houses where three out of the four Beatles grew up — modest, with the surprising exception of "Mendips," John Lennon's childhood stucco house, by far the largest, most middle-class of the bunch. We then took in the former registry office where John married his first wife, Cynthia, in the summer of 1962; the former site of Blackler's department store, where the teenaged George Harrison served briefly as a junior electrician; and the Britannia Adelphi Hotel, where the Beatles stayed during the Liverpool premiere of *A Hard Day's Night.*

But an hour later, Sam had snapped only a half dozen desultory pictures. He'd taken photos of St. Peter's Parish Church, where the teenaged John Lennon and Paul McCartney first met at a Sunday-afternoon fete; Philharmonic Hall, where Paul McCartney rehearsed his 1998 symphonic opus, *Liverpool Oratorio;* the former site of the Liverpool Children's Hospital, where Ringo, at age six, spent six months convalescing after peritonitis (Ringo was sick a lot as a kid); and the two elephantine churches that stand in opposition on either end of Hope Street in downtown Liverpool, one Anglican, the other Roman Catholic. Otherwise, he kept his disposable camera tucked between his knees.

As Hillary drove us around, I couldn't shake the feeling that Sam wasn't with us. His body was, but he, the boy who'd fallen in love with the Beatles, whose conversation was dominated once by John, Paul, George, Ringo, Martha the sheepdog, Ravi Shankar, and the Blue Meanies, was disappearing. So far this trip, I'd been enjoying Sam's company too much to fret over his lack of interest in the Beatles sights we'd seen.

But now Sam's distractedness seemed to be hardening into indifference. Inside the car, Sam responded politely but unenthusiastically to Hillary's attempts draw him out. "Must apologize for the car, Sam," she called into the back seat. "Car wash was closed. That's life, right?" A vaporous "Yeah." Twenty minutes later, "There's number three Gambier Terrace, Sam, where John lived while at the Art College. John is said to have slept in a coffin. Can you imagine *that*, Sam?"

"Yes," he answered. "I mean, no. I mean, why would anybody want to do that?"

It wasn't Hillary's fault. "I've a wonderful job for fulfilling people's dreams," she told me sincerely as we pulled out of the train station. And clearly she knew everything there was to know about the Beatles. Song snippets, birth times, the precise dates of marriages and funerals? Hillary knew it all, and Sam, with the respect and perhaps cunning that you give to an experienced competitor, let her take center stage.

Her expertise extended to setting up her car's tape deck to play the Beatles song germane to wherever we found ourselves. In front of John's house, yards from where his mother was killed, the melancholy strains of "Julia" floated out of the speakers. "A Little Help from My Friends" serenaded us as we paused in front of the row house at number 9 Madryn Place, where Ringo was born. The tour was young, and I was sure there was more coming.

But when Hillary parked across the street from the Empress Pub in the Liverpool neighborhood known as the Dingle, Sam didn't move. "Sam, we've got to mobilize," I said, and reluctantly, he climbed out of the back seat and joined Hillary and me on the sidewalk. The grimy industrial odor that had assailed my nostrils earlier was a lot stronger here. The streets were damp and unnaturally quiet, and the few cars passing by made faint swishing sounds. A gull cried overhead. A sweatlike mist flattened my hair to my temple and made the back of my neck feel clammy and unwashed. Except for a young Middle Eastern woman limping along with her head down, the neighborhood was deserted.

As we made our way past the Empress Pub, whose exterior adorns the cover of Ringo's first solo LP, *Sentimental Journey*, Hillary filled us in on some local background. Richard Starkey moved into Admiral Square in 1954, a few months after his mother's second marriage to a London painter and designer named Harry Graves, whom most Beatles biographers credit with turning Ringo on to both the best and worst of late-1950s American life—D.C. comic books, film magazines, candy, bubble gum—which Graves used to smuggle home from his office at the U.S. Air Force base at Burtonwood. That same year, Ringo contracted a cold that developed into pleurisy of the lungs, resulting in half a year's convalescence at a children's hospital on the Wirral (rhymes with "squirrel") Peninsula across the Mersey River from Liverpool.

By now, we were standing in cramped, rain-slicked Admiral Square. With its white-painted brick, apricot detailing, and sheer curtains, number 10 was unremarkable, except for one thing: a doll was staring down at us from the second-floor window. Hillary was just telling us about the Starkey family's decision to move out of number 10 (they couldn't face another day of using the outdoor bathroom in full view of fans perched on the back fence) when good, even spectacular, luck struck. The frail, elderly inhabitant of number 10 noticed us on the sidewalk, opened the front door, and beckoned us inside. Hillary gazed at me questioningly. I turned to Sam. "Are you up for it?"

"Sure," he said softly.

If number 10 was unremarkable on the outside, inside it was startlingly eccentric. The little living room where Sam and I were standing smelled of talcum powder, soup, and its own damp heating system. The old wallpaper was faintly dotted with pinecone clusters and dominated by a wall clock that captured the bent, greasy figure of Elvis Presley behind its two black hands.

Stuffed animals peered from chairs and under couch pillows. They lolled around the room, matted and pop-eyed. One, a bear, wore a scarf around its neck with *Indiana University* scrawled across it. Next to it, a pigtailed doll sat splay-legged across a pillow beside a second doll, whose coal-black face, saucer eyes, and crayon-red mouth would make any socially conscious person squeamish.

"This is *really* where Ringo grew up?" Sam whispered. "Yeah," I whispered back, "from the age of fourteen until he became a Beatle."

Margaret (Hillary introduced us at the door) was dressed in a wrinkled housedress and battered slippers. She looked as if she'd just awoken from a long nap. She and Hillary evidently knew each other from previous tours, and as they began catching up, Sam hung back politely in the doorway. He'd never seen living quarters as small and barren as these before, and he kept sneaking glances at me, his eyes puzzled and even concerned. I could tell he was also intrigued by the dolls and the stuffed animals. I was so fixated on them myself that I registered the click and sudden flash of his camera only when it was too late. Both Hillary and Margaret glanced up, surprised.

"Sam," I murmured, "you shouldn't take pictures of people's houses without asking them first." He looked immediately abashed. "Sorry about that," I added to Margaret, but she gazed back at me without understanding.

"Do those stuffed animals all belong to her?" Sam whispered when we were back outside, "or were they her kids'?"

So far, the collusive hiss was our preferred conversational style here in Liverpool. "I think they must be hers," I whispered.

"Poor dear," Hillary broke in. Sensing an invitation to continue, she told me that Margaret had once lived on the streets of Liverpool, that is, until number 10 Admiral Square became available. Her friendliness and eagerness for company had gotten her into trouble a few months earlier, when she'd opened up her door to two guys who roughed her up and made off with her purse.

The thought of someone beating up this nice old woman heightened the unease I'd felt since arriving in Liverpool. The Beatles' hometown wasn't at all what I'd imagined. The band may have set their memories and early impressions to music, but the place that inspired those memories was disconcertingly real: a sore, proud, insolent, rough-hewn, banged-up, soccer-crazy industrial Northern English port city. Our tour hadn't done much to alter my unrest. The weather may have been to blame — the rolling clouds, the spasming rain, the gulls in a dark sky. It may have been the sodden sidewalks or the empty churches and grounds. It may have been the sprawl and emptiness of the Liverpool docks, made soulless through a well-meaning restoration, or the apprehensive quiet of the Dingle.

More likely, though, it had to do with Sam.

We climbed back inside the car and Hillary drove onward. Even when we came to a stop across the road from the Strawberry Field gates, and the song's eerie first chords cued up, Sam appeared neither excited nor its opposite.

"Oh, my God, this is *amazing*," I said to Hillary.

For once, the song and what inspired it intersected, at least in my head: Strawberry Field was a haunting place, as eerie and desolate as its melody. Not that you could see much: just a set of big, dark red gates, coiled into sunbursts and curlicues, and beyond and through the metal, a stretch of neglected grass. In John Lennon's time, Strawberry Field referred to the local Salvation Army Children's Home; Lennon used to come here as a boy accompanied by his Aunt Mimi.

"D'you want to scoot out onto the sidewalk and take a picture, Sam?" Hillary asked. "One for the photo books?"

"No, thank you."

She wouldn't give up. "Maybe you'd like me to take a picture of you and your dad, standing out in front? Bring it home to Mum, show her where you've been on all your travels?"

"Ummmm . . ." Sam seemed pained. The smile he gave her belonged to an athlete playing injured. "Actually, I can just do it like this." He swung the hand holding the camera out the open back-seat window. It was the third or fourth picture he'd taken this way. At first, it had seemed jaunty, and a good way to avoid getting soaked, but now his cocked arm seemed less insouciant than apathetic.

"Oh, let's go for it, Sam," I said cheerfully. "Even if you don't want to pose for a picture, *I* do."

Up close, the two stone posts were intricately penciled with graffiti of the "Beatles Forever" variety. Sam was wearing the reluctant, freeze-dried smile he used for school photos, nurses, and girls. I knelt down and put my arm around him, and Sam put his around me, slumping into me melodramatically. Hillary took up position on the near sidewalk, pointing Sam's camera at us. "Ready, steady . . . ?" she called over. Sam wobbled beside me as I beamed like the CFO of a Fortune 500 company enjoying record profits. I could hear the raindrops clipping against Sam's hair as the shutter went off. It was two-thirty in the afternoon, but the camera's automatic flash went off.

We got back in the car and continued on. Drab blunt streets, rows of postwar housing. Empty sidewalks, abandoned parks.

Clearly, we were heading toward the tour's pinnacle; the road signs gave it away early. In a narrow street, Sam and I hopped out of the car, moments after "Penny Lane" cued up on the tape player. "This is the place," Hillary enthused. "That's where 'the shelter in the middle of the roundabout' used to be." She gestured at the bar-restaurant now standing there, which bore the name Sgt. Pepper's Café. She added that fans had stolen Penny Lane street signs so often that the city had painted the two words onto buildings.

And then Sam and I stepped out into Penny Lane. It was an anonymous, commercial street. I craned my neck. Hardly the chaotically lighthearted, frantically well-traveled place I'd expected. It was an urban thoroughfare going about its business. Where were the "blue suburban skies"? Where were the pretty nurses "selling poppies from a tray"? Where were the barber, the banker, and the fireman? Where were the images and characters that had filled my head as a boy? Where *was* my childhood? The cheerful song with its soaring piccolo trumpet now tooting out of the car seemed to mock my naïve expectations.

Was this really all there was? Was it my fault? Penny

Lane's fault? The song's? Paul's? Or was it nobody's fault? Was "fault" the wrong word here? After a brief photo in front of the barbershop mentioned in the song, Sam and I climbed back inside Hillary's car. I felt too exposed standing there, waiting for something. But what? Beatles songs I felt I knew better than my best friends were being reduced, one after another, to the mundane—an old gate, a tired street, a shop with a barber pole in front of it, a smoky pub, a curtained house, an empty roundabout. This was getting depressing. Worse, I had a paranoid suspicion that the locals knew exactly why I'd come to Liverpool, and felt sorry for me.

We drove around the city a little while longer, stopping briefly across the road from various other Beatles-related sites—a primary school John once attended, the graveyard where Julia Lennon is buried, and the Jewish cemetery where Brian Epstein lies. By now it was nearly three-thirty. Sam looked exhausted, his eyes half closed. He was only nine years old, after all. He couldn't do this all day.

Hillary dropped us off near the Cavern Club, the cellar pub where the Beatles made their local debut, and 273 subsequent appearances. "Cheers," she called out and waved good-bye.

Sam and I made our way down little, winding Mathew Street, past a statue of John Lennon that bore no resemblance to its subject. Brian Epstein had dropped into the original Cavern Club one day at lunchtime and, disregarding the advice of the Beatles' then manager Alan Williams "not to touch them with an effing barge pole," signed on as their manager. That shrine was bulldozed in the early sixties to make room for a parking lot. By 1994, Liverpool realized its error and rebuilt a spiffy exact replica using bricks left over from the original, or so it was claimed.

Though I wasn't crazy about the idea of paying my respects to a synthetic Cavern Club, Sam and I had come a long way, so we trundled down the stairwell and into the basement. Among other things, the original Cavern Club was famous for its smell — smoke, sweat, and rotting vegetables from the street's enormous storage bins — but this version just smelled a little musty.

Cavern Club II was empty. There was a small, lit stage in the back, casually arrayed tables and chairs. A young bartender was polishing beer steins with a rag. "Hullo," he called out. "Can I help?"

"No, thanks," I said.

Up the staircase and back out into the eggplant-colored Liverpool afternoon. I noticed a store selling Beatles mouse pads, T-shirts, watches, CDs, and other memorabilia, and we wandered in. "Sam, see anything you want?" I asked.

Sam was fingering a Yellow Submarine snow globe, but at the sound of my voice, he replaced it on the shelf and briefly surveyed the store. "I don't think I'd really *use* anything," he said after a moment. "I'd buy it and it would just sit there."

"OK," I said, and we left the store and Mathew Street. I noticed that Sam didn't seem remotely sad, or put off, by his first day in Liverpool. Now that he'd been released from Hillary's car, he had his energy back. We returned to our hotel in the gathering dusk. In the morning, we'd take a taxi back to the suburb of Allerton, to visit Paul McCartney's childhood house.

Liverpool felt less grim the next morning. The sun was high, the Mersey River looked green, not gray, and flecks of light jiggled happily on its surface.

When Sam and I pulled up outside number 20 Forthlin Road, I spied a strangely familiar man on the front lawn snapping a photo of two smiling, overweight tourists. He looked, I realized, like a McCartney. The same hair, the same soulful eyes, the same boyish features. I knew that Paul's younger brother, Mike, still lived just across the Mersey, on the Wirral Peninsula. Had Mike stopped by his old haunts?

"I'm John," the man said, putting out a firm hand. "I take care of things at number twenty Forthlin Road."

A classic 1950s council house, number 20 was simple, a brick rectangle with two floors, a narrow chimney, and a small, tangled garden in front. Still, because of what the Beatles became, the house, which almost precisely resembled the other houses on the block, exuded a rough-hewn shimmer, a charisma. In a proud, injured city, it stood out. I couldn't help but wonder foolishly if there wasn't something magical about the insides. Was the water that flowed from the faucets special? Or could someone like Paul McCartney have grown up in a gravel pit and accomplished what he did?

John led Sam and me up the walkway to the front door while informing us of the house rules. We were allowed forty-five minutes inside; during that time, we could go wherever we wanted, except behind obviously locked doors. We should feel free to sit on the furniture if we wished. John asked only that we didn't plop ourselves down on the lawn chair in the back garden, as a heavyish visitor had done just that a few months earlier and broken the frame. No photo taking was permitted, either. When Sam asked why, John explained that Mike McCartney had lent his photos of early life at number 20 Forthlin Road to the National Trust on the condition that no one infringe upon his copyright.

John handed us two contraptions, the kind you see in museums, with a tape player and headphones, that offered prerecorded blurbs about each room. "I'll be around and about if you have any questions," he said. "Give a shout if you need anything."

"This is really cool," Sam said, putting on his headphones and going into the living room. According to my shiny pamphlet, the National Trust maintained the house precisely as it had looked when Paul was a boy. A black-and-white TV. A lamp with a frilly shade. Vaguely Oriental wallpaper—willow trees with looping branches and tiny Asian figures—covered over with Mike McCartney's photographs of Paul's father, Jim, relaxing after a day's work, a deliberately blurred one of a teenaged Paul and John hunched over their guitars, Paul perched with calm defiance atop a piano. Jim McCartney looked like a good man, kind. We listened to Mike McCartney's voiceover, recalling the first day John visited the McCartney household, dressed in skin-tight drainpipe pants and sporting a pair of "sidies." Mike almost always referred to Paul as "our kid."

The adjoining area, a small dining room without a table, had a glass case sparsely filled with early Quarry Men and Beatles memorabilia—45 rpm records, a Beatles button, early concert programs. Next to the dining room was a small, spotless kitchen, crowded with chubby, milk-white, 1950s-vintage appliances, including a primitive washer and dryer with a pair of metal tongs to transfer the clothes from one into the other. Simple shelves above the stove held an assortment of jars for spices, flour, sugar, as well as two black-handled tin pots. A door at the rear of the kitchen led out to a small, enclosed, green lawn, a detached shed, and a toilet.

Sam sidled up to me. "Dad," he said in a low voice, "what does the guy who lives here *eat*?"

"I'm not sure," I whispered. "Maybe he goes out to restaurants a lot."

On the upstairs landing, two locked doors faced each other as if in the throes of an ancient staring contest. Evidently, this was where John the caretaker kept his personal belongings. The larger of the two open bedrooms, which faced the back lawn, was filled with a half dozen more framed photographs, including one of a shirtless teenaged Paul and another of Paul's uncle Albert, whose name, at least, had made an appearance in a song on Paul's solo album *Ram*. Through the black headphones, Mike's voice now recalled how "our kid" used to shimmy up the drainpipe and let himself in through the open window whenever he would lock himself out by accident.

Paul's bedroom was tiny and square and utterly anonymous. A linoleum floor, a single neatly made bed, a corner armchair, a window with gauzy curtains. Here he'd dreamed up the lyrics to "When I'm Sixty-Four" and written "I'll Follow the Sun," both when he was a teenager. I glanced out the window at what Paul saw as a boy: nothing but another row of brick council houses.

Back downstairs in the living room, we took seats on the McCartney family couch. The house had good vibes. It felt like a happy place—loving, protective, what you want in your childhood home. I remembered once reading how close-knit the McCartney family was, with a parade of extended relatives dropping by to lend a hand after Paul's mother died. This feeling was reflected in the cozy rooms, the chair pushed up companionably beside the fireplace grate. After a while, Sam and I retraced our steps, surveyed the back lawn, and ended up back in the living room, gazing at the tiny people frolicking on the wallpaper.

It wasn't a big house. Forty-five minutes felt generous. The rest of the time the National Trust allotted its visitors, presumably, was to intensely imagine the past: John and Paul practicing music in the living room; scribbling lyrics down on school notebooks; Paul's father home from the Liverpool Cotton Exchange and standing at the stove, cooking for his two sons. But it wasn't easy. I stared at the exact spot where, according to the audiotape, John and Paul sat and practiced their earliest songs, and felt a wave of despair when my imagination wouldn't cooperate.

John the caretaker rejoined us. "You have fifteen minutes left," he said. "I have time to answer any of your questions."

"I have a question," I blurted out. "Is it just coincidence that you look so much like Paul McCartney?"

He'd been told that before, he replied. But no, he was no relation to the McCartney family. Back when he was applying for the job at the National Trust, he was frankly concerned that his resemblance to Paul would work against him and that tourists might think the National Trust had installed a Paul look-alike at number 20 Forthlin Road for commercial reasons. "It's not a terribly gimmicky place," John remarked dryly, "the National Trust." In his opinion, he looked more like George than Paul. "It's the fangs," John clarified. With a finger, he peeled back his top lip, exposing a dagger-tipped side tooth. "See here? George had fangs, too."

Had he ever met Paul? Sam wanted to know. "He dropped here about a month ago. Came right to the door and knocked. My luck not to be here at the time." He'd met Paul before, of course, years ago. A stand-up guy, disarmingly regular, down-to-earth.

Sam stepped forward uncertainly. "Um, don't you get *hungry* sometimes?" John hesitated and then ushered us into the kitchen. Taking a ring of keys from his pocket, he unlocked the door of a narrow supply closet, revealing a microwave oven, soup cans, and boxes of pasta and rice. "I have pretty much everything I need," he told Sam. "Even the stove works here." To demonstrate, he flicked the burner knob on and off. Now he keyed open a second cabinet, revealing a boom box, CDs, and more food. "But I don't let people go into my bedroom upstairs," John concluded. "There are some places you have to keep for yourself, for privacy's sake, you know?"

As we were on our way out, John mentioned that he was working on a memoir chronicling his years as the custodian of Paul's house. He'd been keeping copious daily notes. For instance, there was the incident that took place a couple of years after John Lennon died. A man showed up on the house tour wearing a white suit, his hair bunched in a ponytail, looking uncannily, miraculously, like John Lennon. "It was the strangest thing," said the caretaker. The Lennon look-alike had crept silently through the downstairs and the upstairs, never uttering a single word, even when John addressed him.

"D'you think it might have been John's ghost?" Sam asked helpfully.

John threw him a mournful glance. "I don't think so." By now, he'd pulled out a scrap of crushed, ink-scribbled paper from his pants pocket. Later that evening, he told me, he'd transcribe his notes inside a logbook he kept. "I already have a title for the book," he said shyly. "Can you guess it? I'll give you a hint: it's the name of a song."

"'My Love'? 'Maybe I'm Amazed'?" I shook my head. "I can't guess."

"'The Long and Winding Road'?" Sam tossed out.

John smiled sadly. "Here's a clue—what happens when a knock comes on the front door?"

"'Too Many People'?" I guessed. That was a song from *Ram*.

"'Arrow through Me'?" Sam tried. That was from *Wings*. John shook his head at our guesses.

"Um . . ." Sam said, "you tell us."

"No, I'll tell you what happens: I open the front door, and I . . ." John looked at me with understated pride.

Finally I got it. "Let 'em in."

"That's it," John said. "There's the title of my book right there."

There was a long silence. "I guess you should maybe let us out now," I said at last.

Sam and I spent the rest of the day roaming around Albert Dock. We paid a visit to Liverpool's crown Beatles exhibit, known as "The Beatles Story," situated in a restored building on the Albert Dock. Here, visitors paid a hefty fee to wander through a suite of rooms, each one offering one or more dioramas of notable scenes from Beatles history—a radio station, a facsimile of the Cavern Club, the Yellow Submarine. Finally you spilled out the other end into an extravagant but nearly empty Beatles-themed gift shop.

Like most of the other Liverpool exhibits I'd seen, "The Beatles Story" felt listless and dated. Even with people passing through them, the rooms felt deserted. But it also put something into perspective for me. The cloudy sky, the drumming rain, the lifeless statuary around Liverpool that bore no resemblance to any Beatle, the discomfort and disappointment I'd felt since our train arrived in Liverpool: all these things had their roots in a simple, inevitable fact. Time was passing, nudging the Beatles backward into history, further into anecdote. The Beatles, through no fault of their own, were getting colder, quainter. They were freezing into a story, an inert, fuzzy myth. They were becoming untouchable. Time was taking care of that. The closer Sam and I got to them—and Liverpool was about as close, geographically, as you could get—the farther away it seemed we'd ended up.

Why had we come here anyway? I kept trying to remind myself. To knock down the distance left between the Beatles and us. I realized how unrealistically high my expectations were. I'd come to Liverpool hoping to gain an ultimate understanding of the Beatles. I'd come here hoping to be transformed—scraped raw, turned inside out, shocked, spooked, flipped over. I'd wanted Penny Lane to come to life. I'd wanted the spooky gates at Strawberry Field to live for me as they'd lived for John Lennon. I'd wanted to collide against something living. Something messy. Sloppy. Breathing. Was that too much to ask?

"So, Dad, what are we doing to do now?" Sam asked as we exited "The Beatles Story." His arms were tightly crossed against his chest, and he was jumping up and down to stay warm.

We had four more hours before night crashed down on us. The tickets I'd paid for included free admission to all the Albert Dock exhibits. "How about we go on a ferry ride?" I said brightly.

From the water, Liverpool looked distinguished, its handsome federal buildings lined up along the dock. The ferry made two stops across the Mersey on the Wirral Peninsula, at Seacombe and Woodside, a distance of about a mile away from the Royal Liver Building that straddled the Liverpool docks. Considered the most picturesque of Merseyside's five boroughs, Wirral played a superficially historic role in the Beatles' lives. It was here the band played for the first time wearing suits; here where Cynthia, the first Mrs. John Lennon, grew up in comparative poshness; here where, undoubtedly, the four Beatles came in their youth to swim at the New Brighton and Wallasey beaches. The Wirral appeared to fulfill a symbolic role for Liverpudlians as the right side of the tracks: where you aspired to live if you'd made something of yourself.

Then the ferry turned back to the Albert Dock.

Fate took place here, I kept telling myself, almost through gritted teeth. The seemingly chance intersection of four childhood friends coming together to form the best, most famous group in the world — *here. In Liverpool.* These smoky buildings, these blistered chimneys, this clipping rain had everything to do with who the Beatles were, and who they became. The trip wasn't a complete bust. Even if the Beatles had rejected Liverpool (and among the Beatles only Paul was known to be fiercely loyal to the place, giving generously to local interests), at least Sam and I had seen and heard and touched and smelled firsthand what they'd left behind.

Sam spent most of the trip hooked over a railing, his

slicker flapping, the breeze whipping his hair back. I sat on a bench, gazing backward at the Liverpool skyline. It struck me that Liverpool didn't really know what to do with the Beatles. Not yet, at least. Certainly, Liverpool had no interest in modeling itself as Beatles Central. Despite the few souvenir stores and low-key statuary, I couldn't help but notice the striking absence of Beatles-themed commerce around town. Sure, there was Strawberry Fashion, and a muffler replacement store promising car owners "a clean machine," but that was about it.

The ferry bumped lightly into the Albert Dock, and Sam and I filed down the stairs to the crackling strains of "Ferry Across the Mersey," by Gerry and the Pacemakers, a Liverpool band contemporary with the Beatles. I turned to Sam. "Wouldn't it be awful to be one of Gerry's Pacemakers?"

"Why?"

"You grow up wanting to be a famous musician but you find yourself fated to have been born in the same city where the Beatles were from. Imagine trying to launch your band, Gerry and the Pacemakers, when you have the Beatles to contend with."

"Oh, yeah," Sam said, trying to digest this exquisite morsel of wisdom, which, if taken to its logical limit, was a parental mandate to stay in bed for the rest of your life, because what was the point? "Right."

"Wait," I said. "That was a dumbish thing to say."

"I know," Sam replied with a little laugh.

As we headed back to our hotel, Sam said, "It smells a little, but parts of it are nice. I had fun today." He seemed to be wrestling with a thought. "Dad," he said at last, his eyes vague, slightly lowered.

"Uh-huh?"

"When I was younger, I thought 'Strawberry Fields' was a field of strawberries."

Recalling his own naïveté—his own childhood—Sam smiled.

"Really?" I said.

"Yeah. And I thought 'Penny Lane' was a place where there were pennies growing out of the ground. Or else it was a place where people threw pennies for good luck, and then made wishes."

My nearly ten-year-old son gazed evenly at me, flinching a little under the specking rain. He was, offhandedly, making a point: that was then, this is now. I felt a pang in my stomach, though all of it made sense, didn't it? The soldiers he'd brought along with him to England, his general floppiness in London and inside Hillary's car. He was inching away from the Beatles and toward a new preoccupation, one that had lifted him from the drowsy half-life of satiety.

"So you're feeling kind of *off* the Beatles?" I heard myself say.

"What do you mean off the Beatles? You mean not liking them?"

I nodded.

Sam gazed at me confusedly. "Of course I like the Beatles. What are you talking about?"

"But you just said, 'When I was little.' So I got confused."

"Dad, I *do* like them." Sam hesitated. "I just like other things, too. You're interested in a lot of different things, too. It doesn't mean I've stopped liking them." He paused. "Dad, it's not a *choice* here."

I reminded him of the time he'd first heard *Abbey Road* in the car, and how we'd reenacted the crossing on a pathway to the beach; how "Octopus's Garden" had lodged in his head that first night, and his delight when I told him the protagonist of "Maxwell's Silver Hammer" bopped people on the head. About the day the Paul McCartney letter showed up on our dining room table, about the weeks we'd spent poring over album covers for Paul-is-dead clues, and the glimmers Sam picked up inside songs: crickets chirping, bubbles blowing, a door slamming, a half-empty bottle of Blue Nun rattling on the speakers. This last one seemed to puzzle him.

"Wait, what did I say?" When I repeated the Blue Nun sound affect from "Long, Long, Long," Sam still looked baffled. "I guess I *sort* of remember saying that. Or reading that. Wait—what's Blue Nun again?"

I couldn't help but feel a little dashed. It was done, is what he was saying. Two years of childhood Beatlemania— it sounded like an infection—was now trickling to an end. Not only that, but Sam had begun to forget other things, too: remarks, conversations. This period would someday be reduced to a hazily lit, generally good-natured place called *childhood*.

"Hey, don't worry about it," I said finally. "The same thing had happened to me when I was your age."

"What did?"

"I moved on. Got interested in other bands." The Beatles were, I recognized finally, a portal. They were your first group. They were your first girl, your first oyster, your first black tie, your first good kiss. They introduced you to a few random pieces of life and eventually to other music, other bands. "After the Beatles, I went on to the—Sam, don't tell anybody this—the *Monkees.* The Rolling Stones, sort of. Stevie Wonder. Then much harder stuff. But you always go *back* to the Beatles, Sam," I went on, "always. It's the strangest thing. The Beatles never go away. You have these" —I tried to think of the word—"*marathons.* You hear one song, so you take down *The White Album* again, or *Sgt. Pepper,* and it starts you up all over again. See, forty years after they broke up, they're still the best group in the world."

And here was another thing I'd realized during our trip to England, and even earlier. Sam and I didn't need the Beatles anymore. Not the way we'd needed them two years ago. The distance between us was long gone. Just as the Beatles were a portal to other music, they were a portal to a friendship between my son and me.

Sam took my hand as we headed back to the hotel, then released it hurriedly when he spotted a sidewalk cafe. "So, you want a cup of coffee?" I asked him.

"Could I have a cappuccino, please," Sam said to the boy behind the counter. Before I could reach for my wallet, he'd already laid down a two-pound coin. When I tried to overrule him, he insisted, "No, Dad, it's my treat. You've been paying for everything this trip."

His cappuccino came, and he picked up a plastic spoon and stirred it soberly. "Wow," I said. "Wow. Remember when you told me you'd never, ever drink coffee when you got older?"

"When did I say that?"

"I can't remember. Some time, a while ago."

"I like coffee," he said. "It makes me feel smarter, and warmer."

For the next half-hour, we chatted about various things —his school, what books he was reading, what movies he was most eager to see when we got home, his friend Alex. It began to pour. Umbrellas shot up, a parade of crows.

"Dad, I think you're in a grumpy mood," Sam said presently.

"No, I'm not."

"I can tell. You think you can fool people, but I can tell. Your voice starts squeaking, and you look like you're paying attention, but you're not."

He might be too young to understand what I was about to say, though probably he wasn't. "You're right," I said. "I think I feel a little confused. Being here makes me feel kind of old."

"Dad, you *are* old."

"Thanks."

"Welcome."

"I mean—what—I'm forty-two, right? It's just a little disappointing being here," I explained, "disillusioning. I think I imagined something totally different. Like Penny Lane. You know Busytown, in the Richard Scarry books, with Hilda the Hippo, and Lowly the Worm and the rest?" Sam nodded. "I sort of pictured Penny Lane looking like that. You know, crowded, thriving, everybody dancing around . . ."

Sam's voice was patient, measured. "But the Beatles wrote the songs *after* that."

"What do you mean?"

"They were just the names they saw growing up, like Penny Lane and Strawberry Field. Dad, all that was back in the *1950s*. You weren't even born then. Then the Beatles turned them into songs. And songs make you think of whatever you want to think. The Beatles just made them up."

He was right. It was obvious. He'd understood something that I knew perfectly well took place all the time—in songs, in books, in movies. You took stuff from your own and other people's lives, then stuck a vest and a mustache on them. You gave them a pipe, spiky hair, a new name. In the end, they bore only the dreamiest resemblance to life. What people called "art" rose up from the slammed doors and scrambled eggs of day after day, from the mailman's comment, the chestnuts clopping down onto the car hood, the flowers across the street that looked like poppies. As ever, creating anything was an opportunistic act, no surprises there. The trick was making other people think it was good art.

My son had had to remind me of this. It brought us both back to life. "I mean, think about it," I said. "Paul's mother dies. And so he writes—"

" 'Let It Be,' " Sam broke in.

"John's mother dies, and he writes—"

In unison—"'Julia.'"

"And 'My Mummy's Dead,'" Sam added. "And 'Mother.'" He stood suddenly, nearly upsetting his cup. "Dad, Strawberry Field is—like—a *gate*."

"Penny Lane is a *street*," I said. "But you have to understand, they don't *exist* either."

"What do you mean?"

"The songs are what Penny Lane and Strawberry Field *should be*. In a perfect world, I mean. Couldn't John and Paul honestly say that they *created* Penny Lane and Strawberry Fields? That neither one of them *really* existed before they were songs?"

"Wait." Sam paused. "I *think* so. Wait, I just saw it in my head, and then it went away."

We weren't just seeing old gates, old roads, old doorways, old row houses, I told him. We were browsing ideas, images, speculations, the pre-bones of songs. I was wrong: our being here was as intimate as the Beatles permitted anybody who wasn't a Beatle.

The songs. We'd had them with us from the start, and Sam knew this. I felt like Odysseus mulling over "home." Dorothy, clicking her heels and she was there, home all along. Everything we needed, and had come for—the mythical proximity I'd come to Liverpool in search of—was there already, inside Sam's and my head: "I Saw Her Standing There." "Misery." "Anna (Go with Him)." "Chains." "Boys." "Ask Me Why." "Please Please Me." "Love Me Do." "P.S. I Love You." "Baby It's You." "Do You Want to Know a Secret?" "A Taste of Honey." "There's a

Place." "Twist and Shout." "It Won't Be Long." "All I've Got to Do." "All My Loving." "Don't Bother Me." "Little Child." "'Till There Was You." "Please Mr. Postman." "Roll Over Beethoven." "Hold Me Tight." "You Really Got a Hold on Me." "I Wanna Be Your Man." "Devil in Her Heart." "Not a Second Time." "Money (That's What I Want)." "A Hard Day's Night." "I Should Have Known Better." "If I Fell." "I'm Happy Just to Dance with You." "And I Love Her." "Tell Me Why." "Can't Buy Me Love." "Anytime at All." "I'll Cry Instead." "Things We Said Today." "When I Get Home." "You Can't Do That." "I'll Be Back." "No Reply." "I'm a Loser." "Baby's in Black." "Rock and Roll Music." "I'll Follow the Sun." "Mr. Moonlight." "Kansas City/Hey, Hey, Hey." "Eight Days a Week." "Words of Love." "Honey, Don't." "Every Little Thing." "I Don't Want to Spoil the Party." "What You're Doing." "Everybody's Trying to Be My Baby." "Help." "The Night Before." "You've Got to Hide Your Love Away." "I Need You." "Another Girl." "You're Going to Lose That Girl." "Ticket to Ride." "Act Naturally." "It's Only Love." "You Like Me Too Much." "Tell Me What You See." "I've Just Seen a Face." "Yesterday." "Dizzy Miss Lizzie." "Drive My Car." "Norwegian Wood (This Bird Has Flown)." "You Won't See Me." "Nowhere Man." "Think for Yourself." "The Word." "Michelle." "What Goes On." "Girl." "I'm Looking through You." "In My Life." "Wait." "If I Needed Someone." "Run for Your Life." "Taxman." "Eleanor Rigby." "I'm Only Sleeping." "Love You To." "Here, There and Everywhere." "Yellow Submarine." "She Said She

Said." "Good Day Sunshine." "And Your Bird Can Sing."
"For No One." "Doctor Robert." "I Want to Tell You."
"Got to Get You into My Life." "Tomorrow Never Knows."
"Sgt. Pepper's Lonely Hearts Club Band." "With a Little
Help from My Friends." "Lucy in the Sky with Diamonds."
"Fixing a Hole." "Getting Better." "She's Leaving Home."
"Being for the Benefit of Mr. Kite." "Within You Without
You." "When I'm Sixty-Four." "Lovely Rita." "Good Morn-
ing Good Morning." "Sgt. Pepper's Lonely Hearts Club
Band (Reprise)" "A Day in the Life." "Magical Mystery
Tour." "The Fool on the Hill." "Flying." "Blue Jay Way."
"Your Mother Should Know." "I Am the Walrus." "Hello
Goodbye." "Strawberry Fields Forever." "Penny Lane."
"Baby You're a Rich Man." "All You Need Is Love." "Only a
Northern Song." "All Together Now." "Hey Bulldog." "It's
All Too Much." "Back in the U.S.S.R." "Dear Prudence."
"Glass Onion." "Ob-La-Di, Ob-La-Da." "Wild Honey
Pie." "The Continuing Story of Bungalow Bill." "While
My Guitar Gently Weeps." "Happiness Is a Warm Gun."
"Martha My Dear." "I'm So Tired." "Blackbird." "Piggies."
"Rocky Raccoon." "Don't Pass Me By." "Why Don't We Do
It in the Road?" "I Will." "Julia." "Birthday." "Yer Blues."
"Mother Nature's Son." "Everybody's Got Something to
Hide Except Me and My Monkey." "Sexy Sadie." "Helter
Skelter." "Long, Long, Long." "Revolution." "Honey Pie."
"Savoy Truffle." "Good Night." "Come Together." "Some-
thing." "Maxwell's Silver Hammer." "Oh! Darling." "Octo-
pus's Garden." "I Want You (She's So Heavy)." "Here
Comes the Sun." "Because." "You Never Give Me Your

Money." "Sun King." "Mean Mr. Mustard." "Polythene Pam." "She Came in through the Bathroom Window." "Golden Slumbers." "Carry That Weight." "The End." "Her Majesty." "Two of Us." "Dig a Pony." "Across the Universe." "I Me Mine." "Dig It." "Let It Be." "Maggie Mae." "I've Got a Feeling." "One after 909." "The Long and Winding Road." "For You Blue." "Get Back." "Day Tripper." "We Can Work It Out." "Lady Madonna." "Hey Jude." "Don't Let Me Down." "I'm Down." "Paperback Writer." "Long Tall Sally." "Yes It Is."

Plus, I'm sure I'm forgetting some.

EPILOGUE

ONCE, my wife remarked with surprising fervor how grateful she was to have lived at the same time as the Beatles. From childhood to college to marriage, the group had always engendered a near-impossible happiness in both of us. Over the past two years, my debt to the four of them, which was already colossal, had found a new, unexpected means of expression: they handed me a relationship with my son. As partial repayment, I'd given them possession of Sam. Now, gently and without fanfare, they'd handed him back to me.

The irony of Sam maxing out on the group in their hometown of Liverpool was lost to no one, especially Sam. Back at home, he confided to me that he'd agreed to come to London and Liverpool "so that you and I could take a trip together, Dad. I didn't really care that much about seeing Beatles stuff. I went to Liverpool because *you* wanted to go to Liverpool."

For Sam, the Beatles weren't at all "over." He'd absorbed them, the way I had at his age, and moved on. The obsession part of it was over. The Beatles were now a given, there if he ever wanted or needed them. The final, best thing they left him with? A standard of what "great" is, or can be.

We still play them a lot around the house. "Yeah, I love the Beatles," Sam will respond casually, if the subject comes up. Last summer, I treated everyone to Paul McCartney's solo concert at Madison Square Garden and was amazed by the number of preteen and teenaged kids mouthing the Beatles songs along with Paul. Now and again, Sam will take down one of his worn-out Beatles factoid books and fall asleep reading it. At breakfast, he might throw out an impossible question. (How many non-Beatles movies are there in which a Beatle appears? Answer: sixteen.) On the long car trips we take, he, or one of his sisters, will inevitably end up requesting *Abbey Road,* or *Rubber Soul,* or *A Hard Day's Night.*

But Sam's memory is clouding. We were listening to Norah Jones on the radio the other night, and I said, "OK, for ten points, who's Norah Jones's father?"

Sam thought for a moment. "Michael J. Fox?"

"Ravi Shankar!" I said.

Sam looked quizzical. "Wait . . . who's that again?"

These days, the Beatles are a background to other things we do together: tennis playing, bike riding, Frisbee throwing, swimming, traveling, and cooking (last week I taught him how *not* to make a roux). At eleven, nearly twelve, Sam still plays the piano, still fences, and next year he begins seventh grade. He's old enough now to babysit for his sisters. Several times, I've had to remind him of his strength. If he's fallen asleep downstairs, I can no longer lift him from the couch with any ease. His shoulders are getting broad; his hands large; a classmate, a girl, called the house the other day, but she left no name.

I love him, and his two sisters, more than anything in the world.

A few months ago, Sam said, "Dad, you *have* to come into the living room."

Why? He wanted to introduce me to a new animated cartoon he'd bought on DVD. The show was *SpongeBob SquarePants,* and it was about the adventures of a flaky sea sponge, a dim-witted starfish named Patrick, and a Texas-born squirrel named Sandy. "Dad, will you stay? There's this part—" and Sam sprang down onto the floor, poised to release the Pause button. "Don't go," he commanded. "Stay."

I hung in the doorway as the show resumed. Out of the corner of my eye, I saw Sam shooting glances at me. Was I smiling? Laughing? Did I look bored? Impatient? "Don't you think this is good?" Sam asked. "The writing and everything?"

Though SpongeBob wasn't the Beatles, I understood its meaning to him. It was hard to believe there might be a message wrapped and buried in a sea sponge, a starfish, or a squirrel, just as it was probably hard for my own father to find one in a walrus, a rich man, or a doctor named Roberts. But there was one. Sam was offering up a piece of his generation, and himself in it, as distinct from mine, and me. This was all his. He wanted me to approve of it. He wanted me to love it. He was saying, *We can show you things, too.* So I smiled and I sat down and I stayed.

ACKNOWLEDGMENTS

I would like to thank my wife, Maggie, who first saw this as a book, and who accompanied Sam and me on this adventure every step of the way; Lily and Susannah, for their patience, understanding, great hearts, and wit; Bill Clegg, who was there when I took the road less traveled and fielded the results spectacularly; and Eamon Dolan, genius editor, whose pen took aim at places way beyond the text.

SOURCES

Needless to say, there have been scads of books written about the Beatles. In the course of discovering the group again with Sam, I found myself tucking in with, and in some cases rereading, the following Beatles biographies, oral histories, and anthologies. Sam's list—containing a list of books that appeal to adults and kids—follows mine.

Beatles. *The Beatles Anthology.* New York: Chronicle Books, 2002.

Bennahum, David. *The Beatles after the Break-Up.* London: Omnibus Press, 1981.

Brown, Peter, and Steven Gaines. *The Love You Make: An Insider's Story of the Beatles.* New York: Signet Books, 1983.

Davies, Hunter. *The Beatles.* New York: W. W. Norton & Co., 1968.

Doggett, Peter. *Abbey Road/Let It Be* (Classic Rock Albums series). New York: Schirmer Books, 1998.

Gambaccini, Paul. *The McCartney Interviews: After the Break-Up.* London: Omnibus Press, 1996.

Jones, Ron. *The Beatles Liverpool: The Complete Guide.* Wirral: Ron Jones Associates, 1991, 2000.

Kozinn, Allan. *The Beatles.* London: Phaidon, 1995.

Miles, Barry. *Many Years from Now.* New York: Henry Holt, 1997.

Sources

Norman, Philip. *Shout! The Beatles in Their Generation.* New York: Fireside/Simon & Schuster, 1981.

Porter, Richard. *The Official Abbey Road Café Guide to the Beatles' London.* London: Abbey Road Café, Ltd., 2000.

Ryan, Susan, ed. *Rooftop Sessions Fiction Digest, Volume 2: The Finest in Beatles-Related Fiction.* Rooftop Sessions and Susan Ryan, 2002 (available at www.rooftopsessions.com).

Sam's Favorites

Aldridge, Alan, ed. *The Beatles Illustrated Lyrics.* Boston: Seymour Lawrence/Houghton Mifflin, 1969.

Dowdling, William. *Beatlesongs.* New York: Fireside/Simon & Schuster, 1989.

Harry, Bill. *The Beatles Encyclopedia.* London: Virgin Publishing, 1992.

MacKenzie, Maxwell. *The Beatles Every Little Thing: A Compendium of Witty, Weird, and Ever-Surprising Facts about the Fab Four.* New York: Avon Books, 1998.

Patterson, R. Gary. *The Walrus Was Paul: The Great Beatle Death Clues.* New York: Fireside/Simon & Schuster, 1996, 1998.

Spignesi, Stephen J. *The Beatles Book of Lists.* New York: Citadel Press/Carol Publishing, 1998.

Toropov, Brandon. *Who Was Eleanor Rigby . . . and 908 More Questions and Answers about the Beatles.* New York: HarperCollins, 1996.

Turner, Steve. *A Hard Day's Write: The Stories Behind Every Beatles Song.* New York: HarperPerennial, 1994.